The International Criminal Court

This book examines the main features of the International Criminal Court (ICC) from a political science and international relations perspective. It describes the main features of the Court and discusses the political negotiations and the ongoing clashes between those states that oppose the Court, particularly the United States, and those that defend it. The second aim of the book is to understand the negotiations on the establishment of the ICC as an example of how international decision-making is influenced by global civil society. Finally, it asks whether such global civil society influence is really to be welcomed as a democratic or ethical contribution to international politics.

Established in 2002, the ICC can be considered a revolution in international law and in the conduct of international relations, for two reasons. First, the ICC is a milestone in the ongoing transition towards an international legal order that is less based on state sovereignty and more oriented towards the protection of all citizens of the world from abuse of power. Second, the input of global civil society in the process which led to the establishment of the Court has been almost unprecedented in international treaty negotiations. In this volume, Marlies Glasius describes the fascinating political negotiations that led to this type of court and the main features of the ICC including:

- the crimes covered by the Court;
- the role of the prosecutor;
- the jurisdiction regime;
- the gender aspects of the Court;
- the Court's position on weapons of mass destruction.

This book will provide an introduction to the International Criminal Court for non-lawyers, in particular to students of political science and international relations.

Marlies Glasius is a Lecturer in Management of Non-Governmental Organisations at the Centre for Civil Society and a Research Fellow at the Centre for the Study of Global Governance, London School of Economics and Political Science. From 2000 to 2003 she was managing editor of the *Global Civil Society Yearbook*.

Routledge Advances in International Relations and Global Politics

1 **Foreign Policy and Discourse Analysis**
France, Britain and Europe
Henrik Larsen

2 **Agency, Structure and International Politics**
From ontology to empirical enquiry
Gil Friedman and Harvey Starr

3 **The Political Economy of Regional Co-operation in the Middle East**
Ali Carkoglu, Mine Eder and Kemal Kirisci

4 **Peace Maintenance**
The evolution of international political authority
Jarat Chopra

5 **International Relations and Historical Sociology**
Breaking down boundaries
Stephen Hobden

6 **Equivalence in Comparative Politics**
Edited by Jan W. van Deth

7 **The Politics of Central Banks**
Robert Elgie and Helen Thompson

8 **Politics and Globalisation**
Knowledge, ethics and agency
Martin Shaw

9 **History and International Relations**
Thomas W. Smith

10 **Idealism and Realism in International Relations**
Robert M. A. Crawford

11 **National and International Conflicts, 1945–1995**
New empirical and theoretical approaches
Frank Pfetsch and Christoph Rohloff

12 **Party Systems and Voter Alignments Revisited**
Edited by Lauri Karvonen and Stein Kuhnle

13 **Ethics, Justice and International Relations**
Constructing an international community
Peter Sutch

14 **Capturing Globalization**
Edited by James H. Mittelman and Norani Othman

15 **Uncertain Europe**
Building a new European security order?
Edited by Martin A. Smith and Graham Timmins

16 **Power, Postcolonialism and International Relations**
Reading race, gender and class
Edited by Geeta Chowdhry and Sheila Nair

17 **Constituting Human Rights**
Global civil society and the society of democratic states
Mervyn Frost

18 **US Economic Statecraft for Survival, 1933–1991**
Of sanctions, embargoes and economic warfare
Alan P. Dobson

19 **The EU and NATO Enlargement**
Richard McAllister and Roland Dannreuther

20 **Spatializing International Politics**
Analysing activism on the internet
Jayne Rodgers

21 **Ethnonationalism in the Contemporary World**
Walker Connor and the study of nationalism
Edited by Daniele Conversi

22 **Meaning and International Relations**
Edited by Peter Mandaville and Andrew Williams

23 **Political Loyalty and the Nation-State**
Edited by Michael Waller and Andrew Linklater

24 **Russian Foreign Policy and the CIS**
Theories, debates and actions
Nicole J. Jackson

25 **Asia and Europe**
Development and different dimensions of ASEM
Yeo Lay Hwee

26 **Global Instability and Strategic Crisis**
Neville Brown

27 **Africa in International Politics**
External involvement on the continent
Edited by Ian Taylor and Paul Williams

28 **Global Governmentality**
Governing international spaces
Edited by Wendy Larner and William Walters

29 **Political Learning and Citizenship Education under Conflict**
The political socialization of Israeli and Palestinian youngsters
Orit Ichilov

30 **Gender and Civil Society**
Transcending boundaries
Edited by Jude Howell and Diane Mulligan

31 **State Crises, Globalisation and National Movements in North-East Africa**
The Horn's dilemma
Edited by Asafa Jalata

32 **Diplomacy and Developing Nations**
Post-Cold War foreign policy-making structures and processes
Edited by Justin Robertson and Maurice A. East

33 **Autonomy, Self-governance and Conflict Resolution**
Innovative approaches to institutional design in divided societies
Edited by Marc Weller and Stefan Wolff

34 **Mediating International Crises**
Jonathan Wilkenfeld, Kathleen J. Young, David M. Quinn and Victor Asal

35 **Postcolonial Politics, the Internet and Everyday Life**
Pacific traversals online
M. I. Franklin

36 **Reconstituting the Global Liberal Order**
Legitimacy and regulation
Kanishka Jayasuriya

37 **International Relations, Security and Jeremy Bentham**
Gunhild Hoogensen

38 **Interregionalism and International Relations**
Edited by Heiner Hänggi, Ralf Roloff and Jürgen Rüland

39 **The International Criminal Court**
A global civil society achievement
Marlies Glasius

The International Criminal Court

A global civil society achievement

Marlies Glasius

Routledge
Taylor & Francis Group
LONDON AND NEW YORK

First published 2006
by Routledge
2 Park Square, Milton Park, Abingdon, Oxon OX14 4RN

Simultaneously published in the USA and Canada
by Routledge
270 Madison Ave, New York, NY 10016

Routledge is an imprint of the Taylor & Francis Group

Typeset in Sabon by
Keystroke, Jacaranda Lodge, Wolverhampton
Printed and bound in Great Britain by
TJ International Ltd, Padstow, Cornwall

British Library Cataloguing in Publication Data
A catalogue record for this book is available from the British Library

Library of Congress Cataloging in Publication Data
Glasius, Marlies.
The International Criminal Court : a global civil society achievement / Marlies Glasius.–1st ed.
p. cm. – (Routledge advances in international relations and global politics)
"Simultaneously published in the USA and Canada."
Includes bibliographical references and index.
1. International Criminal Court. 2. International criminal courts.
3. Civil society. I. Title. II. Series.
KZ6311.G53 2005
345′.01–dc22
2005000835

ISBN 0–415–33395–4

Contents

Illustrations

Figures

Map

Preface

The Rome Statute for an International Criminal Court, which was adopted on 17 July 1998, provides for the establishment, in The Hague, of an international court that can prosecute individuals, from common soldiers to heads of state, for genocide, war crimes, and crimes against humanity. The International Criminal Court was established on 1 July 2002. It can be considered a revolution in international law and in the conduct of international relations, for two reasons.

First, the International Criminal Court (ICC) is a milestone in the ongoing transition towards an international legal order that is less based on state sovereignty and more oriented towards the protection of all citizens of the world from abuse of power. Second, the input of global civil society in the process which led to the adoption of this Statute has been almost unprecedented in international treaty negotiations, rivalled only by its contribution to the Landmines Ban Treaty, concluded six months earlier.

While the history of the ICC has been described before, these accounts tend to concentrate on the official history. This book will discuss how the two phenomena, the development of a more people-empowering international rule of law and the emergence of a global civil society, interacted with each other to produce the ICC.

The book has two aims. On the one hand, it will provide an introduction to the ICC for non-lawyers, in particular students of political science and international relations. It describes the main features of the Court: the crimes it covers, the role of the prosecutor, the jurisdiction regime, the gender aspects and its position on weapons of mass destruction. It discusses the political negotiations that led to this type of court, as well as the ongoing clashes between those states that oppose the Court, particularly the United States, and those that defend it.

Its second aim is to understand the negotiations and struggles surrounding the establishment of the ICC as an example of how international law-making and the building of global institutions are influenced by global civil society. The input of organisations and individuals from civil society in the process of establishing the ICC was unprecedented. This book uses the negotiations on different parts of the ICC Statute as a hook to discuss the merits and difficulties of this involvement of what can be broadly termed global civil society in international law-making and institution-building.

The opening chapter highlights the informal initiatives that paved the way to the ICC. It shows how the biggest advance in international law of the past decade, the establishment of an International Criminal Court, was from the outset a global civil society project. It will also discuss the current status of the Court and the active opposition to the Court from the United States.

The next chapter introduces the global civil society actors who became involved in the ICC project. It describes the simultaneous growth of the 'Like-Minded' group of states and the NGO Coalition for an International Criminal Court. It discusses what kinds of groups and individuals took an interest in the ICC, from which parts of the world they came and what concerns they had, and examines the working methods of the Coalition.

Chapter 3 describes how, despite fierce opposition from certain states, the Court got an independent prosecutor who can launch his or her own investigations, and makes the case that this was mainly due to global civil society influence.

Chapter 4 on the other hand describes how, despite the efforts of 'like-minded' states and representatives of global civil society, secret end-game negotiations led to a restrictive jurisdiction regime: not restricted enough to forestall opposition from the United States, but not wide enough to make the reach of the Court universal. This has since emerged as the Court's biggest problem.

Chapter 5 discusses what emerged as the biggest controversy *within* global civil society with respect to the ICC. Women's groups wanted – and got – many clauses in the Court Statute dealing with gender concerns. Conservative and, particularly, pro-life groups tried to keep the term 'gender', and the crime of forced pregnancy, out of the Statute. This controversy serves as a point of departure for a reflection on who the actors in global civil society are, who participates in international negotiations, and how internal controversies are dealt with.

Chapter 6 describes the largely unsuccessful attempts of a small contingent of peace groups working on the ICC to have the possession and use of weapons of mass destruction defined as a crime under the ICC Statute. This issue brings up strategy issues for global civil society negotiators, as well as again questioning internal decision-making procedures within global civil society.

The final chapter reconsiders and problematises the idea that global civil society makes a 'democratic' contribution to international law-making and institution-building in the light of the experiences in the ICC process. It picks up on issues concerning strategy, internal controversy, the constraints of state-framed paradigms, and representation raised by the foregoing chapters. The chapter ends by making a case that, in certain areas that could be defined as 'global public goods', more international law, with more global civil society influence, is to be preferred over a return to state sovereignty.

This book grew out of a chapter called 'Expertise in the Cause of Justice: Global Civil Society Influence on the Statute for an International Criminal Court', in *Global Civil Society 2002*. After writing the chapter, I felt I had more to say, more to research and, especially, more thinking to do than space and deadlines would allow. I had also noticed that the emerging writing on the ICC was very lawyerly, and that there was a need for a more political book. I would like to thank Routledge for sharing this assessment.

Special thanks go to Peter Baehr and Simone Remijnse, who read and commented on first drafts of every chapter of this book. I am also grateful to the civil society actors and diplomats who made time to let me interview them, especially Bill Pace, who gave me many hours of his time, and to those who responded to e-mail queries. Further thanks go to Helen Durham, who shared parts of her unpublished dissertation with me; Alyn Ware, who commented extensively on Chapter 6 – the conclusions of which he does not share; and Olaf Corry, who commented on the final chapter.

A slightly different version of Chapter 5 has been published as 'Who Is the Real Civil Society? Women's Groups versus Pro-Family Groups at the International Criminal Court Negotiations' in Jude Howell and Diane Mulligan (eds), *Gender and Civil Society* (Routledge, 2004). As such, it was commented on by Jude and Diane, as well as two anonymous reviewers. I gratefully acknowledge their suggestions.

Final thanks go to Mary Kaldor for general support and intellectual inspiration, and to all those who came to listen to the numerous presentations I gave, and debated with me and helped me to clarify my ideas.

Abbreviations

AMICC	American Coalition for an International Criminal Court
ANICC	Asian Network for the International Criminal Court
ASPA	American Service-members Protection Act
BIA	bilateral immunity agreement
CICC	Coalition for an International Criminal Court
ELSA	European Law Students' Association
EU	European Union
FAO	Food and Agriculture Organization
IALANA	International Alliance of Lawyers Against Nuclear Arms
IANSA	International Action Network on Small Arms
ICBL	International Coalition to Ban Landmines
ICC	International Criminal Court
ICFTU	International Confederation of Free Trade Unions
ICJ	International Commission of Jurists
ICRC	International Committee of the Red Cross
ICTY	International Criminal Tribunal for the former Yugoslavia
ILC	International Law Commission
LMG	Like-Minded Group
NAM	Non-Aligned Movement
NGO	non-governmental organisation
PrepCom	Preparatory Committee
SADC	Southern African Development Community
UN	United Nations
WTO	World Trade Organization

1 A universal criminal court

The emergence of an idea

The idea of an international criminal court

The revolutionary nature of the idea of an international criminal court lies in the combination of the two elements, international and criminal. Both international law and criminal law have been around for centuries; one might even argue, millennia. International law regulated relations between governing entities, but even before the emergence of modern states, the punishment of crimes was always the privilege of the ruler. What should happen if the acts of the ruler him- or herself could be considered, by some moral standard, criminal, has exercised philosophers and inspired revolutions all over the world. The Dutch rebels united in the Union of Utrecht, for instance, legitimised their secession from the Spanish crown in 1581 as follows:

> It is apparent to everyone that a Prince of the realm is appointed by God over his subjects, in order to protect them against all injustice, troubles and violence, as a shepherd to protect his sheep; and that the subjects were not created by God in order to serve the Prince as slaves and obey him in all he orders, whether it be godly or ungodly, just or unjust; but the Prince for the sake of his subjects, without which he is no Prince, in order to govern them by right and reason, and champion them and love them as a father loves his children and a shepherd his sheep, who would risk his life to preserve theirs. And when he does not do so, but instead of protecting his subjects, seeks to repress them and take away their old freedoms, privileges, and customs and to order and use them as slaves, he must be considered not a Prince but a tyrant, and his subjects may, by right and reason . . . no longer recognise this Prince, but choose another in his stead to protect them without abuse.
>
> (Plakkaat van Verlatinghe, 1581; translation by the author)

The idea that a ruler's power cannot be absolute, that there must be standards beyond the ruler to protect his or her citizens, has become the foundation stone of international human rights law. But the idea of international criminal law, and an international criminal court, goes a step further. In the extreme case where the ruler commits or condones crimes against his or her people, it takes not only the formulation of norms, but also the administration of punitive justice out of the ruler's hands and up to the international level, even to the point where the ruler him- or herself can be tried on criminal charges. A truly universal criminal court could finally invalidate the cynical dictum (attributed to Stalin) that 'if you a kill a man you are a murderer, if you kill a thousand you are a conqueror'.

For a 'prince' or a modern government, to recognise an international criminal court means to sign away a small but essential part of one's sovereign power in order to protect future citizens against a possible situation where it or its successors become unwilling or unable to prosecute genocide, war crimes, and crimes against humanity committed by their citizens or on their territory. This chapter will discuss where this idea came from, and how it evolved from being considered a utopian pipedream to a serious proposal, and finally into a reality. But first it will devote a few words to the second main subject of this book, global civil society.

The idea and global civil society

Civil society, let alone global civil society, is a confusing term. As even a brief glance at the literature shows, it has many meanings. There are as many definitions of civil society, and global civil society, as there are authors – in fact, there are more: Lewis (2002) extracts four definitions of civil society from the literature on Africa alone, Howell and Pearce (2001: 13–37) juxtapose two versions, and Kaldor (2003: 6–12) gives no fewer than five versions of global civil society.

Nevertheless, this book quite intentionally uses this term, rather than other current ones such as global social movements (Cohen and Rai, 2000), advocacy networks in international politics (Keck and Sikkink, 1998), or global citizen action (Edwards and Gaventa, 2001). First, the choice of 'civil society' to characterise the ensemble of people and organisations I describe in this book: I prefer this precisely because the history of the term 'civil society' is bound up with the notion of rules to protect citizens. The term goes back to ancient Rome (*societas civilis*), but was used particularly in the Enlightenment to express the idea that a ruler did not have a divine right to do with his subjects as he pleased, but rather, that people came together voluntarily and negotiated a hypothetical social contract to form a civil society in which the rights and obligations of the citizens and the ruler were clearly outlined. (See Seligman (1992) for one of the best expositions on Enlightenment thinking on civil society.) With the exception of Kant (1795/1991), the Enlightenment thinkers thought of this rule-bound society only in national terms. However, the post-world war notion of universal human rights, coupled with a thickening network of international rules directly affecting citizens, has given birth to the utopia of a global rule-bound society. Hence, the idea of global civil society is historically connected with the ideas behind humanitarian and human rights law.

However, I want to show in this book that this connection is more than a historic accident without contemporary relevance. Global civil society in the modern sense of the whole of border-crossing, non-profit, non-governmental entities remains intimately connected with the international rule of law. It may be intuitive that the emergence of a global civil society is dependent on the development and observation of the international rule of law. The opposite connection is less obvious, but the history of humanitarian law and human rights law, of which I will describe only a small portion here, has been much more a product of the activities of people outside government than is commonly accepted. Almost every significant treaty in international humanitarian law originates with the International Committee of the Red Cross. In the area of human rights, the idea of a universal declaration came from a small group of lawyers – often political refugees themselves – before the Second World War; the insertion of human rights provisions in the UN Charter was the work of non-governmental organisations (NGOs); and a post-war treaty, the Convention Against Torture, was almost solely the brainchild of human rights NGOs (see Burgers, 1992; Keck and Sikkink, 1998: 85; Clark, 2001: 55–67).

It would be quixotic to believe that international law can come into existence without the backing of states, or overcome the opposition of a majority of states. This has never happened in the past, and whatever one may believe about the erosion of state power through globalisation, it is not possible today. However, it is equally the case that those parts of international law that intend to protect the interests of humanity, rather than the interests of states, do not come about without the involvement of global civil society. While the final authorisation has to come from states, the moral and intellectual impulse to draft such rules inevitably comes out of global civil society.

Second, the choice of 'global', rather than transnational or international civil society. Those authors who prefer the latter terms suggest that 'global' sounds too grandiose; in the sense of something that really brings together people from every part of the globe, it just isn't there, and is not inevitably going to be there either (Florini, 2000; Keck and Sikkink, 1998; Smith *et al.*, 1997). In the empirical sense, they have a point. Some parts of the world are much more linked up than others. There are few links with Equatorial Guinea or rural China.

However, as I have argued elsewhere with two co-authors, while 'global' may overstate what is really out there, 'transnational' understates it. All one needs to be transnational is a single border crossing. In that sense, civil society has been transnational for at least two hundred years. 'Transnational' does nothing to capture the revolution in travel and communications, and also the opening up of many formerly closed societies that has really made civil society much more global in the past ten years than it has ever been before. Moreover, only 'global civil society' can be posed as a complement as well as a counterweight to the process now universally called 'globalisation'. Finally, the term 'global civil society' has a normative aspiration that 'transnational civil society' does not. Just as the term 'human rights' has a universalistic intent that 'civil rights' lacks, global civil society can be seen as an aspiration to reach and include citizens everywhere and to enable them to think and act as global citizens. Some of the literature on globalisation stresses the emergence of a global consciousness, an 'imagined community of mankind' (Shaw, 2000). In this sense, global civil society is an expression of that consciousness even if the participants cannot travel or even use the telephone (Anheier *et al.*, 2001: 16–17).

So what exactly *is* this global civil society? In the *Global Civil Society Yearbook*, we adopted the following working definition: 'global civil society is the sphere of ideas, values, institutions, organisations, networks, and individuals located *between* the family, the state, and the market and operating *beyond* the confines of national societies, polities, and economies' (Anheier *et al.*, 2001: 17). Here, I propose a definition that is a little narrower and much simpler: global civil society consists of people organising to influence their world. Hence, it involves some sort of deliberate getting together, and it is a political definition, excluding people who organise to play darts or make money. It is a descriptive rather than a prescriptive definition: it includes those who (in my view) attempt to influence their world in undesirable directions, or by unpalatable means. The subjective 'their world' suggests that these people are concerned with the world they see themselves as living in, their 'life-world', rather than that they necessarily work on a planetary scale. It also suggests that (global) civil society is a contested terrain (Howell and Pearce, 2001: 234), populated by value-driven actors, but not necessarily with a single harmonious value system: as this book will show, their values sometimes clash.

I intend in this book to explore the relationship between the empirical 'people organising to influence their world' and the normative ideal of a 'global rule-bound society'. However, in order to avoid confusion, I will be using the term 'global civil society' throughout the book only in the former sense, also sometimes referred to as 'actually existing civil society'. The following chapters introduce many of the global civil society actors involved in the ICC process and focus on their background, motivations, methods and influence. It becomes clear that many were motivated by the very fact that a 'global consciousness' was part of their life-world, and this is where the descriptive concept and the normative ideal reconnect.

Origins of the idea

A 'global consciousness' was certainly not the overriding factor in the 1474 trial of Peter von Hagenbach, much cited in the literature as the first 'international criminal trial' for what could today be called charges of crimes against humanity. An *ad hoc* international criminal tribunal of twenty-eight judges from towns in Alsace, the Rhineland and Switzerland, with a presiding judge from Austria, tried and convicted him for murder, rape and perjury, crimes which 'trampled under foot the laws of God and man', carried out during his governorship of the town of Breisach on behalf of Charles, the Duke of Burgundy (Schwarzenberger, 1968: 462–466). However, this trial did not exactly embody the revolutionary features of an international criminal court as outlined above. Who was the rightful 'prince' of the town of Breisach was unclear to begin with: Breisach had been pledged as collateral by the Archduke of Austria to Charles of Burgundy. When it became clear that Charles intended to incorporate this and other towns into Burgundy indefinitely, Austria and a number of allies declared war and retook the city. Whether the judges really formed an international panel is also a matter of opinion: recognition of the independence of the Swiss territories from the Holy Roman Empire (Germany) was in dispute at the time. In form and substance, the trial was more an instance of victor's justice than of the application of universal moral standards: von Hagenbach was severely tortured before the trial, in order to extract confessions which were quite unnecessary, as there were numerous witnesses to his openly committed crimes.

A more significant source of the idea is the proposal made by Gustave Moynier of Switzerland, one of the founders of the International Committee of the Red Cross (ICRC), in 1872. The history of 'international humanitarian law', or 'the law of war', demonstrates how, not just in the late twentieth century, but historically, international law has been much more a product of the activities of people outside government than is commonly accepted. Almost every significant treaty in international humanitarian law originates with the ICRC. The first of these, now superseded by subsequent treaties, was the Geneva Convention for the Amelioration of the Condition of the Wounded in Armies in the Field of 1864. While the Convention was signed by a large number of 'civilised nations' at the time, members of the emerging Red Cross movement found to their horror that it was widely ignored, and that atrocities were committed by both sides, in the Franco-Prussian War in 1870. Many declared the Geneva Convention to be a dead letter, and suggested that the Red Cross should henceforth just concentrate on tending to the wounded, not on drafting rules. Gustave Moynier, a lawyer from Geneva, however, argued that the Convention remained valid, but it needed a complement: the establishment of an international criminal court to deter violations of the Convention, and to bring to justice anyone responsible for such violations. He did not envisage a permanent court. Instead, as soon as a conflict broke out, the warring sides would each choose a judge, and the two would be complemented by three judges from neutral countries. While the panel would pass sentences, the implementation of the sentences would be left to the states themselves (Hall, 1997b; Boissier, 1963: 371–373).

Moynier's proposal undoubtedly had its imperfections: although he did not trust the warring states to punish their own subordinates for war crimes, he believed they would have no objection to carrying out the sentences handed down by the Court he envisaged. Nevertheless, he can be considered the founding father of the powerful and perilous idea of taking the power to judge certain crimes away from (warring) states, and putting it into the hands of an international tribunal. However, enthusiastic as they had been about the original Geneva Convention, states took virtually no notice of this proposal. Fellow international lawyers also responded sceptically to the idea of an international court that would actually mete out sentences, and even the national Red Cross committees reacted with great reserve, so that Moynier was forced to abandon the project (Boissier, 1963: 373–374).

How the idea was kept alive

The International Committee of the Red Cross did continue its work of pushing for the codification of the laws of war, resulting in a set of treaties in 1899 and 1907, collectively referred to as the 'The Hague Conventions', so that when the First World War broke out, there was a solid body of humanitarian law. After the war, the Versailles treaty provided for *ad hoc* tribunals, but only to try military officials of the Central Powers for breaching the laws of war. Germany refused to hand anyone over for prosecution, and the Allies soon lost interest after the German Kaiser had been given asylum in the Netherlands (Von Hebel, 1999: 16; Bassiouni, 1999: 7). The idea of a permanent criminal court was briefly mooted in the League of Nations, but rejected as 'premature' (Von Hebel, 1999: 17; Hall, 1997b).

It fell to individuals and NGOs to promote and develop the idea. In the 1920s, a number of legal scholars wrote proposals for an international criminal court, and in 1925 the Inter-Parliamentary Union adopted a proposal that would enable the existing Permanent Court of International Justice, which adjudicated in disputes between states, to sanction both states and individuals for crimes of aggression. The newly founded Association Internationale de Droit Pénal also backed the idea at its first congress, but the most far-reaching proposal came from the International Law Association, the most august professional body of international lawyers, which had been discussing the idea since 1922 (Ferencz, 1980: 42–45). It held that the 'creation of such a Court is 'not only highly expedient, but also practicable', considering that 'the trial of the nationals of one State by the Courts of another, however fair and impartial in fact it may be, is invariably regarded with suspicion' and that 'experience has shown that trial of war crimes by National Courts, whether of the victor of the vanquished, has almost invariably proved unsatisfactory'. Hence, it recommended that 'the jurisdiction of the Court shall extend to non-military as well as to military offences, whether committed in time of peace or in time of war' (International Law Association, 1927, reproduced in Ferencz, 1980: 255, 257).

However, according to Benjamin Ferencz (later to be one of the prosecutors in the Nuremberg tribunal):

> [D]espite the almost universal support of scholars all over the world, the attempts to persuade decision-makers to create an International Criminal Court proved unsuccessful. . . . The powerful nations of the world were simply not ready for a Court with

> compulsory jurisdiction or a Tribunal to repress international crime.
>
> (1980: 46)

A much more modest proposal, by France, to establish a court to try international terrorists was actually adopted as a treaty by the League of Nations in 1937, but received no ratifications, and never came into force (Von Hebel, 1999: 17–18).

Proposals during the Second World War to set up a permanent international criminal court were rejected in favour of *ad hoc* international tribunals at Nuremberg and Tokyo, followed by Allied national military tribunals to prosecute nationals of the Axis powers. These have been criticised for imposing 'victor's justice', and for convicting people of crimes not previously formulated in laws (Von Hebel, 1999: 20–21). Nevertheless, as Jean-Paul Sartre later put it, 'The Nuremberg tribunal, an ambiguous body, was no doubt born of the right of the strongest; but at the same time it opened a perspective for the future by setting a precedent, the embryo of a tradition' (1968: 42).

Immediately after the Second World War, the international community was briefly united in drafting international rules that would help prevent similar atrocities in future. The Universal Declaration of Human Rights and the Genocide Convention were adopted in 1948. While there were also plans for an international criminal court, it missed the window of opportunity that closed as the Cold War advanced. Two successive *ad hoc* committees actually submitted draft statutes for a court to the UN General Assembly in 1951 and 1953, but the idea was opposed by states on both sides of the Cold War. The International Law Commission, a UN Commission of legal experts, continued to work on a code of crimes against the peace and security of humankind intermittently for the next four decades, but not directly on a court that could try these crimes. (See Von Hebel (1999: 22–27), Hall (1997b) and Bassiouni (1999: 10–15) for a more detailed description.)

Non-governmental organisations like the Association Internationale de Droit Pénal, the International Law Association and the World Federalist Movement kept the idea alive, discussing it regularly in their congresses, and individuals like Benjamin Ferencz, a former prosecutor of the Nuremberg tribunal, as mentioned, and Cherif Bassiouni, an Egyptian law professor in Italy and the United States, spent much of their professional life studying and drafting model statutes and lobbying for an international criminal court.

Meanwhile, the idea received a new, much more radical impetus with the institution of the Russell Tribunals since 1967. The first Russell

Tribunal, or International War Crimes Tribunal as it was properly called, was an initiative in the opposition to the Vietnam War by two august political philosophers, Lord Bertrand Russell and Jean Paul Sartre. It mimicked judicial procedure to the extent that it examined evidence and sought to establish on the basis of the evidence whether – or rather, that – the United States was breaking existing rules of humanitarian law. But it recognised quite clearly that it was powerless, and hence decided not to pass a sentence (Sartre, 1968: 43). The tribunal members were intended as a 'jury' (ibid.: 45) rather than judges, and the purpose was 'to establish, without fear or favour, the full truth about the war' (Aims and Objectives, 1968: 16).

However, as has been described elsewhere, the people involved in the Russell Tribunal did not have a single coherent vision of its procedures and purposes (see Klinghofer and Klinghofer (2002: 103–161) on the acrimonious politics behind the tribunal). Lord Russell expressed the hope that the Tribunal would become a permanent institution, acting as a trial of conscience to crimes committed by the West:

> The International War Crimes Tribunal must do for the peoples of Vietnam, Asia, Africa and Latin America what no tribunal did while Nazi crimes were committed and plotted. . . . The Tribunal must inspire a new morality in the West, in which cold mechanical slaughter will be automatically condemned.
>
> (1968b: 311)

As he had hoped, four more 'Russell tribunals' (not sanctioned by the man himself, who died in 1970) were subsequently held, on repression in Latin America, on human rights in post-war West Germany, on the rights of Indians in the Americas, and on human rights in psychiatry. Lelio Basso, one of the original tribunal members, set up a Permanent People's Tribunal in Rome in 1979, which continues to function (Fondazione Internationale Lelio Basso, website, no date). Russell expressed no interest in an official, state-sanctioned court, possibly because he did not trust states to set up a credible court:

> Powerful states and ruling groups have created institutions such as the United Nations and the World Court, but it is these same states and ruling groups which exploit cruelly the peoples of the world. This is why their institutions cannot echo the demands or the sufferings of the oppressed.
>
> (1968a: 39)

Jean-Paul Sartre, however, was more explicitly inspired by the example of Nuremberg, and saw the tribunal as a precursor and tool towards achieving an official international court:

> [T]he Russell tribunal will have no other concern, in its investigations as in its conclusions, than to bring about the general recognition of the need for an international institution for which it has neither the means nor the ambition to be a substitute, whose essential role would be the resuscitation of the *jus contra bellum* which was still-born at Nuremberg – the substitution of ethical and juridical rules for the law of the jungle.
>
> (Sartre, 1968: 43)

The people's tribunals did not play any direct role in the establishment of the ICC. Indeed, there has been little if any overlap in personnel between the radical intellectuals involved in people's tribunals and the legal scholars drafting model statutes for an ICC. However, the people's tribunals certainly did serve to popularise both the concept of humanitarian law as a living instrument that applied to ongoing conflicts, and the notion that breaching these laws should be considered a 'crime'. In the words of Adriaan Bos, a diplomat who later chaired the negotiations on the ICC Statute, 'the work of that Tribunal . . . did much to prepare the world climate for an international judicial body to try war crimes' (1999: 44).

The idea receives serious attention from states

One of those legal scholars studying the ICC at the same time was the American Robert Woetzel. While he went on to author a number of publications on international criminal law, his biggest contribution to the birth of the ICC was probably his lifelong friendship with Trinidadian fellow Oxford student Arthur Robinson. Robinson was intrigued and inspired by discussions with Woetzel, who was writing a dissertation on the Nuremberg trials (Woetzel, 1960), and went on to attend conferences organised by Woetzel many years later (Robinson, 1999). He also became executive director of the – largely dormant – Foundation for an International Criminal Court, of which Robert Woetzel was President.

When Arthur Robinson became Prime Minister of Trinidad, he used the opportunity to bring together his country's, and indeed the Caribbean region's, preoccupation with the international drugs trade and his own lifelong campaign for an international criminal court by proposing to the General Assembly the 'establishment of an international criminal court with jurisdiction to prosecute and punish individuals and entities who engage in, *inter alia*, the illicit trafficking in narcotic drugs across national borders' (UN, 1989; emphasis mine). Robinson enlisted the help of Robert Woetzel, Ben Ferencz and Cherif Bassiouni in drafting this motion, which cautiously proposed referring the ICC idea 'for study' by the International Law Commission (ILC) in order to avoid outright defeat (Robinson, 1999). While entirely cast in terms of combating the threat posed by drug traffickers, the proposal, and the ensuing General Assembly resolution, suggested that such a court could try persons suspected of international crimes, '*including* persons engaged in illicit trafficking in narcotic drugs' (UN, 1990; emphasis mine). This little word 'including' allowed the ILC to make proposals for a court with much more extensive jurisdiction.

The ILC seized enthusiastically upon this mandate. The Draft Code of Crimes which it had been working on for many years had been a largely academic exercise, but now there was a chance to develop an implementation mechanism that might actually punish perpetrators of these crimes. No one in the Commission considered framing the ICC merely as a drugs court. Instead, the debate focused on whether it should have jurisdiction only over crimes against the peace and security of mankind, or over other crimes as well (ILC, 1993: esp. 30–60).

Parallel to these developments, Professor Cherif Bassiouni assembled an NGO Committee of Experts at one of the two universities where he held a chair, the International Institute of Higher Studies in Criminal Sciences in Siracusa in Sicily, to prepare a draft statute covering all international crimes (Bassiouni, 1999: 16). This was the first of many 'Siracusa meetings', which became an important informal complement to the official meetings over the next eight years.

While getting the court back on the agenda of the ILC was an important step towards realising the idea of the international criminal court, it was by no means a guaranteed road to speedy establishment. Draft legal codes could languish for decades in the rarefied atmosphere of the ILC, far from the political limelight, where years were sometimes spent on the definition of a legal clause. Indeed, stalling was exactly what some countries, including the United States, had in mind when they agreed to refer the idea of an international criminal court to the ILC (Scharf, 1997: 16–17). The ethnic cleansing in Yugoslavia and the genocide in Rwanda, and the subsequent Security Council decisions to establish *ad hoc* tribunals for Yugoslavia and Rwanda, changed all this.

In 1990 and 1991, various Western leaders suggested an international tribunal to try Saddam Hussein and other Iraqi officials, but the idea was not followed up (Cassese, 1996a: 7–11). On 16 May 1991, even before the war in Yugoslavia broke out, the Yugoslav journalist Mirko Klarin wrote an article entitled 'Nuremberg Now' in which he proposed that

> Things being the way they are, would it not be better if our big and small leaders were made to sit in the dock instead of at the negotiating table? And if, with the help of world-famous experts in international laws of war, we had a Nuremberg Trial of our own, no matter how small and modest? Not *when* 'this is all over' but *instead of* whatever might soon befall us.
>
> (1991: 35)

Unfortunately, it was not until more than a year and countless atrocities later, after Omarska and other 'concentration camps' had been found by journalists, that Western leaders took up the idea – in August 1992 at the London Conference on Yugoslavia, a proposal by the French and German foreign ministers to consider the creation of an *ad hoc* criminal court was adopted (Specific Decisions, 1992).

In October 1992, a Security Council resolution authorised the establishment of a commission of inquiry. However, this commission was left with very few funds or cooperation from states, allegedly because both UN officials and the British and French governments felt that an overly zealous response to war crimes would scupper chances of a peace settlement. The first chairman resigned in protest a year later, and the Commission was taken over by the energetic Cherif Bassiouni, who quickly found fifty volunteers and $800,000 from the Soros and the MacArthur foundations, and set up a database on violations at his second home base at DePaul University in Chicago. The Commission also held on-site investigations and exhumations, and one of its members assembled a forty-strong all-female team of lawyers, mental health specialists and interpreters to interview more than two hundred victims and witnesses of rape (Scharf, 1997: 44–48).

Meanwhile, the Security Council adopted a resolution in February 1993 authorising the establishment of an *ad hoc* tribunal, and on 25 May 1993 it unanimously adopted the UN Secretary-General's draft statute. On 8 November 1994, another resolution was adopted, creating the Rwanda tribunal to try those responsible for the genocide of April–July 1994. Both tribunals were, as has been widely acknowledged, established as a fig leaf for the international community, which had not been prepared in either case to commit sufficient troops to prevent the foreseeable crimes against humanity. As has been described elsewhere, both tribunals got off to a slow start, hindered by lack of funds and diplomatic wrangling over appointments, and, in the case of Yugoslavia, deliberately obstructed by those who felt it would get in the way of a peace deal (Scharf, 1997; Beigbeder, 1999: 146–148, 155).

However, by most accounts they were ultimately a qualified success: many high-level officials responsible for the genocide were handed over to the Rwanda tribunal, and the Yugoslavia tribunal eventually succeeded in bringing even Milosevic to justice, although not his henchmen Mladic and Karadzic. The main contribution of the *ad hoc* tribunals to the ICC was that they provided proof that the institution of an international criminal court, overcoming the lack of any precedent and conflicts between different legal systems, was practically possible. They also formed a valuable training ground for those in global civil society who were at the same time pushing for a permanent international criminal court.

In 1993, the ILC invited states to comment on a first Draft Statute for an ICC, and in 1994, at lightning speed by its own standards, it had finished its work. It recommended that states now convene a conference to turn it into a binding treaty (ILC, 1997: 26). Many states that had been hesitant or uninterested began actively to support the establishment of an international criminal court. A number of countries, mainly European and Caribbean, supported the idea of having a conference as soon as possible. However, it was also at this time that the idea of an international criminal court began to meet with serious resistance from some states, including China, Cuba, India, Pakistan and the United States. As a compromise, it was decided that an *ad hoc* committee of state representatives should study and discuss the ILC draft first (UN, 1994). As is discussed in Chapter 2, it was the disappointment with this General Assembly session that led civil society activists to set up the Coalition for an International Criminal Court.

A year later, the *ad hoc* committee was converted into a preparatory committee (PrepCom), the difference being that this committee could actually draft text, and also that it was preparatory to an eventual conference, although no date was yet agreed. One of the things state representatives did in these years was repeat, over and over again, the mantra of 'complementarity': the ICC would not supplant or overrule national jurisdictions, but only step in if national states could not or would not prosecute suspects. Neither of these committees made substantial progress, however, and by this time it was clear that some delegations were just taking part in the discussions in order to delay and weaken the establishment of a court they did not want, while others had major differences of opinion about the kind of court they wanted. However, these years also saw the emergence of a 'Like-Minded Group' of states that were in favour of the swift establishment of a strong court. The Like-Minded Group (LMG) is discussed in more detail in Chapter 2.

At the end of the 1996 sessions, a place and date were set for the conference, a compromise between those states that wanted a conference as soon as possible and those that were in no rush at all: Rome, summer 1998. In 1997, the PrepCom began to meet in working groups instead of plenary meetings, which helped at least to get some text drafted on more technical issues, although all truly controversial matters were still left open.

The idea becomes a reality

By the time of the Rome Conference, which took place from 15 June to 17 July 1998, there was a draft statute which contained more than 1,700 sets of brackets, representing competing proposals for the articles in question (Lee, 1999a: 13). Moreover, about fifty of the state delegations, mainly from developing countries, had not taken part in the preparatory committee meetings at all (Pace, 1999: 193). The first two weeks in Rome were therefore mainly devoted to letting every state have its say, while in the meantime the coordinators of the working groups, largely the same people who had fulfilled this role in the PrepCom sessions, were informally at work trying to forge compromises (Von Hebel, 1999: 36).

After three weeks, on 6 July, a first 'discussion paper' was circulated on the basis of these negotiations and a weekend meeting of 'key' delegates took place at the Canadian embassy. This was followed by a proposal narrowing down the options of the controversial part II of the statute on 9 July, and a final, take-it-or-leave-it package deal in the night of 16 July, the day before the conference was to end. While it looked as if little progress was being made in these last ten days, delegates were involved in a frenzy of secretive talks in search of compromises. Nevertheless, many proponents of the court, both governmental and NGO representatives, began to panic. There was a strong feeling that if the statute were not concluded now, a window of opportunity would be closed, and it might be a long, long time before the same momentum could be reached again (Conso, 1999: 471; interviews Van Boven, Van Troost).

The final session on the Friday evening, 17 July, was very emotional. In response to the final draft, two delegations proposed amendments.

India sought to include the use of nuclear weapons in the definition of war crimes (see Chapter 6) and to deprive the Security Council of the power to refer cases to the court (see Chapter 3). The United States wanted the court to have jurisdiction only with the consent of the country of nationality of the accused (see Chapter 4). Reopening the debate on either of those issues would have meant that the deadline for getting a statute at this conference would be missed, with unforeseeable consequences. Norway introduced a motion to take no action on these amendments, which was overwhelmingly supported. After each of these votes, the delegates broke into applause, which, the second time, transformed into a rhythmic clapping that lasted for ten minutes (Benedetti and Washburn, 1999: 26). At the final, formal plenary session at 10 p.m. on Friday, 17 July, the United States requested that the Statute be voted on, instead of being adopted by consensus. The Statute was adopted by secret vote, with 120 votes in favour, 7 against and 21 abstentions (Lee, 1999a: 23–26).

After the adoption of the Statute, a new PrepCom of state delegates began to prepare for the actual establishment of the court, working on more technical matters like detailed definitions of the crimes in the Statute and rules of procedure and evidence, and the legal relation of the Court with the host country. While most of these negotiations were uncontentious, the United States has, as is discussed in detail later in the chapter, attempted in various ways to exempt its own officials from any possibility of prosecution. This global campaign by the United States continues to be met by an equally forceful counter-campaign by the Coalition for an International Criminal Court, particularly by US-based NGOs. Chapter 4 discusses the jurisdiction regime of the ICC, which is such a thorn in the side of the US administration, and how it was negotiated. The next section of this chapter describes in detail the policies the United States has been pursuing vis-à-vis the Court, and their rationale.

The International Criminal Court officially came into existence in July 2002, two months after sixty countries had ratified the Statute. At the time of writing, ninety-nine states have ratified the Statute. However, the Court did not start functioning until the autumn of 2003, after the prosecutor and judges had been elected and other essential staff appointed.

At the time of writing, no indictments have been issued and no trial proceedings commenced, but the Court is examining two situations which may lead to prosecutions. In July 2003, soon after his election, the prosecutor announced that he had received several communications from NGOs and individuals regarding the situation in the Democratic

Republic of Congo, and in particular in Ituri, and that he would follow the situation closely. He said that he was prepared to seek permission from the pre-trial chamber to start investigations (see Chapter 3), but that he would prefer a referral by the government of the Democratic Republic of Congo. In April 2004, such a referral was made ('Prosecutor Receives Referral', 2004). In January 2004, the government of Uganda referred the situation in northern Uganda, where the Lord's Resistance Army, led by Joseph Kony, operates, to the ICC ('President of Uganda', 2004). The Court began actively to investigate the situation in July. However, at the time of writing it is uncertain whether the prosecutor intends to initiate prosecutions over the situation in Uganda, as concerns have been raised that at the present time they might obstruct peace negotiations (Women's Initiatives, 2004). In October 2004, Burundi made known its intention to refer to the Court, after an internal investigation, the massacre that took place in the refugee camp of Gatumba on 13 August (UN, 2004). It therefore appears likely that, rather against the expectations of civil society activists (see Chapter 3), the first prosecutions will, in fact, derive from state referrals.

Opposition to the idea

The role of the United States during the negotiations on the Statute has been ambiguous. The Clinton administration vouched support for the ICC, and, as this book makes clear, its representatives were very actively involved in the negotiations. However, that involvement meant working very hard to create the kind of Court that the United States wanted. As is discussed in Chapter 4, the United States influenced the provisions on the crucial issue of jurisdiction, but yet the final outcome was not acceptable to it: it left a small but essential loophole in a state's complete sovereignty over its citizens. It was determined that the Court could try a suspect if either (a) the state of his own nationality, or (b) the state where the alleged crime took place had ratified, or given *ad hoc* consent. The second option made it possible for someone whose state of nationality had rejected the Court (for instance, the United States) still to end up before it if the crimes had been committed elsewhere (for instance, on a military mission). According to its complementarity principle, the ICC would always prefer to give priority to domestic prosecution, but the Court itself, not the state in question, would determine whether a state was 'unable or unwilling' to pursue a serious trial.

This, to drive a crack into the wall of sovereignty behind which individuals aligned with the state can shield their misdeeds (albeit a much smaller crack than civil society actors had hoped), had always been one of the driving forces behind the idea of the Court. It was needed precisely because in the extreme circumstances where there is a suspicion of war crimes, crimes against humanity or genocide, states cannot always be trusted to take their own decisions regarding the prosecution of their citizens, because they may be implicated in the acts of those citizens. Yet this was exactly what the United States took issue with: the idea that an international body could decide whether it was willing or able to prosecute its own citizens. To the United States, that was an intolerable infringement of its sovereignty. It has explained time and again that making nationals of non-party states subject to potential prosecution is 'an indefensible overreach of jurisdiction', and, more specifically, that it is

> simply and logically untenable to expose the largest deployed military force in the world, stationed across the globe to help maintain international peace and security and to defend U.S. allies and friends, to the jurisdiction of a criminal court the U.S. does not recognize.
>
> (Scheffer, 1999: 20, 18)

It may seem peculiar to single out the United States here, when there are other states that equally dislike this aspect of the ICC. However, while other states have opposed perceived infringements on sovereignty during the negotiation leading up to the adoption of the Statute, they have been satisfied merely not to ratify the treaty and to stay away from further negotiations. The United States is the only state to date that has pursued an active policy of opposing the Court.

The Clinton administration initially attempted to use the detailed post-1998 negotiations on cooperation with the Court to effectively amend the Statute to exempt officials from non-party states (read: American soldiers) from any possibility of prosecution. In 1999, it tried to get an interpretation accepted by the new PrepCom that would exempt 'official acts' carried out abroad from territorial jurisdiction (Wedgwood, 2001: 201).

After this failed, in March 2000, and surrounded by intense lobbying, it informally introduced a proposal related to article 98.2 of the Statute, which states that 'The Court may not proceed with a request for surrender that would require the requested State to act inconsistently with its obligations under international agreements.' The United States proposed an interpretation of this article that would include new obligations, emanating from new international agreements. More specifically, it proposed that since the Court itself would need a 'relationship agreement' with the United Nations, this agreement could include a provision exempting personnel carrying out acts 'under the overall direction' of non-party states from surrender to the Court (Wedgwood, 2001: 205; Pace and Schense, 2001: 705). In response, the '[r]epresentatives of the like-minded states and NGOs in the UN basement conference rooms . . . were able to coordinate an informal multilateral cold-shoulder' (Wedgwood, 2001: 207, n. 54). In the next PrepCom in June, another rule was proposed with a slight change in language. The NGO coalition did a 'virtual vote count' which showed that 87 per cent of the states that took the floor were against adoption of the rule (Pace and Schense, 2001: 705). Nonetheless, the rule was adopted in order to leave the way open for a possible accommodation of the United States in the UN–ICC relation. No compromise was reached, however.

Against this background, Bill Clinton took a peculiar step on 31 December 2000, his last day in office: he signed the ICC Statute. In international law, signing a treaty is normally an indication of the intention to ratify after parliament has been consulted. However, Clinton (2000) made it clear that the signature was meant to keep the United States in the negotiation process, but he did 'not recommend that my successor submit the Treaty to the Senate for advice and consent until our fundamental concerns are satisfied'. He need not have worried: after this the opposition started in earnest, both in Congress and in the new administration.

In May 2000, the American Service-members Protection Act (ASPA) was first introduced in the House of Representatives. Intended to shield members of the US armed forces and other official personnel from the jurisdiction of the ICC, the Act includes prohibitions on any form of US cooperation with the ICC and a prohibition on military assistance to states parties to the ICC; and, most controversially, it authorises the US President 'to use all means necessary and appropriate to bring about the release of any person described in subsection (b) who is being detained or imprisoned by, on behalf of, or at the request of the International Criminal Court'. On the basis of this final provision, NGOs have dubbed it 'The Hague Invasion Act' (Human Rights Watch, 2002). After a tortuous legislative history, held up at one point because discussion was scheduled for 11 September 2001, the Act was passed, in amended form, by both the Senate and House of Representatives, in May 2002. According to the American Coalition for an International Criminal Court (AMICC), the Act as finally adopted is:

an odd and tortured piece of legislation whose impact is hard to assess. . . . It is the outcome of several contradictory forces: a determination shared with the Administration by House and Senate leadership to make a strong statement of ideological hostility to the ICC, the Administration's resolve to preserve in full the President's constitutional powers in international relations, and some congressional resistance to the Act – especially in the Senate. ASPA can best be understood as three stacked layers:

- The first is the original text that gave the President a few very limited waivers, mostly for sanctions on friendly countries.
- The second layer, dropped right on the first, consists of waivers at the will of the president on all of the operative provisions of the bill. The Administration insisted on these to protect the president's constitutional privileges.
- The last layer on the top of the stack was language added by Senator Dodd that essentially reverses the effect of ASPA by authorizing the US government to participate in a wide-range of international justice efforts:

  Nothing in this title shall prohibit the United States from rendering assistance to international efforts to bring to justice Saddam Hussein, Slobodan Milosevic, Osama bin Laden, leaders of Islamic Jihad, and other foreign nationals accused of genocide, war crimes or crimes against humanity.

  (AMICC, website, no date)

In the same month, May 2002, the Bush administration wrote to the United Nations to 'unsign' the ICC treaty. While unprecedented, unsigning a treaty is not unlawful (Bradley, 2002), and the United States did thereby make it unmistakably clear that it did not intend to support the ICC.

One month later, the United States attempted to insert in a Security Council resolution to renew the UN peacekeeping mission in Bosnia, language that would shield peacekeepers from non-party states from the jurisdiction of the ICC. Having failed to do so, it vetoed the resolution on 30 June 2002, the day before the ICC Statute came into being. After twelve days of negotiating, Resolution 1422 was unanimously adopted by the Security Council (UN, 2002a). It deferred for twelve months any investigation or prosecution by the ICC relating to UN peacekeepers whose state of nationality is not a party to the ICC, and expressed an intention that the resolution be renewed annually (UN, 2002b). A year later, the resolution was indeed renewed as Resolution

1487, albeit after an open meeting in which a number of states raised objections, and with abstentions from France, Germany and Syria (UN, 2003).

At the same time, the United States pursued another avenue to shield its personnel from possible prosecution, related to its wide interpretation of article 98.2: it began to negotiate bilateral non-surrender agreements. The first country to sign such an agreement with the United States was Romania. It had ratified the ICC in April 2002, and signed the agreement in August 2002. This has prompted the European Union to adopt a common position, stating that '[e]ntering into US agreements – as presently drafted – would be inconsistent with ICC States Parties' obligations', but also providing guidelines for more narrowly drafted agreements that would, among other things, ensure national investigation and prosecution of persons requested by the ICC (GAERC, 2002). Apparently, agreements along these lines were not acceptable to the United States. No further agreements were concluded between the United States and EU member states, or EU candidate members. Romania has refused to ratify its agreement on the basis of the EU position (CICC, 2004a).

Seventeen more states are known to have signed bilateral immunity agreements (BIAs) in 2002, and at least fifty-three states did so in 2003. There may be further agreements: figures by the State Department suggest that some have been concluded in secret (United States, 2004). Some of these states, including India, Israel and Pakistan, are non-states parties, happy to strengthen their immunity from the Court with reciprocal agreements. Others, such as Georgia, Sierra Leone and Uganda, are states parties, but nonetheless concluded reciprocal agreements. Most states have signed non-reciprocal agreements, however. In many cases, the United States threatened to withdraw military aid under ASPA if no agreement was signed, and Colombia, Fiji and various Caribbean countries signed only reluctantly, after aid had actually been suspended.

On the other hand, forty-five states have publicly refused to sign BIAs, and as of 15 July 2004, twenty-three states had not signed despite losing US aid (CICC, 2004b). At that date, only seven countries had definitely signed such agreements since January 2004 (CICC, 2004a). Many countries reported as being 'under pressure' in 2003 appear not to have gone through with the agreement, suggesting that, possibly, the US administration has either eased the pressure or become less effective.

The fate of the UN resolution granting immunity to peacekeepers from non-ICC member states in 2004 points in the same direction: in the wake of the Abu Ghraib scandal, and while the United States was seeking to get a resolution on Iraq passed, various members of the Security Council (according to one source, as many as eleven) expressed the intention to abstain on the ICC resolution. The United States therefore decided to drop its efforts to seek renewal (Deen, 2004).

However, after the 2004 election the campaign against the ICC appears to have been reopened. In Congress, the 'Nethercutt Amendment', initially defeated, has been adopted in December 2004. It could lead to the withdrawal of further economic aid from countries which refuse to sign BIAs, including anti-drugs and human right and democracy programmes in Latin America, peace and reconciliation programmes in Cyprus and Northern Ireland, and various programmes in South Africa and Jordan (AMICC website).

US opposition to the International Criminal Court is likely to continue, at least for the coming few years. However, the significance of this 'war' for the functioning of the Court should not be overestimated. It is primarily symbolic. Even without any BIAs, it would have been unlikely that any prosecutor would attempt to pick on US troops as possible suspects, even if there were evidence that they might have committed crimes under the jurisdiction of the ICC. Undoubtedly, many would like to see the US military prosecuted for war crimes committed in Iraq. But Iraq has not ratified the Statute for an International Criminal Court, so the only way such a case might legally come to the Court would be through referral by the Security Council. Naturally, there will be no such referral. More surprisingly, the United States has, after protracted negotiations, abstained from a Security Council Resolution referring the situation in Darfur to the ICC, paving the way for an investigation in Darfur.

Meanwhile, the prosecutor appears to be quietly getting on with investigations in Central Africa, with the approval of the states in question. The real test of the viability of the ICC is not whether it can weather US hostility in the short term. There is nothing to suggest that the United States is a major threat to the operations of the Court. The real test will be whether, in the fullness of time, it will be able to take up cases in which its most powerful supporters are implicated – future situations that resemble, for instance, a Srebrenica or an Operation Turquoise.

2 The global civil society campaign

This chapter discusses the emergence of the Like-Minded Group (LMG) of states and the simultaneous growth of the civil society Coalition for an International Criminal Court (CICC), and their interactions. It examines the kinds of global civil society actors that became involved in the negotiations over the ICC, the issue areas they represented, where they came from and why they were interested in the Court. Then it discusses the methods and forms of action of global civil society actors in their campaign for an international criminal court. Finally, the nature of relations between state officials, especially of the Like-Minded Group, and civil society actors is discussed.

Two coalitions for an international criminal court

The Like-Minded Group

The results of 1994 session of the General Assembly, which decided on further study of the ILC draft in an *ad hoc* commission rather than a diplomatic conference, caused certain state representatives to fear that a conference leading to the adoption of a Statute might never happen. As a result, an informal coalition of states that wanted in the first instance to push for a conference began to emerge in 1995. It became known as the 'Like-Minded Group' (LMG) of states. It originally consisted of maybe ten or fifteen representatives to the General Assembly's sixth (legal) committee, who were also friends. It included Argentina, Canada, Norway and the Netherlands, and its aim was to push for a date for a diplomatic conference, and aim for a Court as effective as possible, with wide definitions of crimes, and a simple complementarity regime (interview Von Hebel). There was an immediate connection with civil society in that '[r]epresentatives of civil society in those countries also exercised considerable influence in pushing governments towards a strong, independent court, principally through the actions of non-governmental organizations' (Kirsch and Holmes, 1999: 8).

The LMG grew continually in number, reaching a membership of sixty-two countries by the time of the conference in Rome (Schabas, 2001: 15). While it was an official grouping in the sense that its membership was known, the LMG mainly operated informally, adopting four 'cornerstone positions' only on one occasion, in December 1997 – and even then these were not put into any official statement (Benedetti and Washburn, 1999). These four were:

> inherent jurisdiction over war crimes, genocide, crimes against humanity and aggression, whether committed during armed conflict between States or internally within nations; a defined and constructive relationship with the UN Security Council which preserves the independence and impartiality of the Court; an independent prosecutor able to initiate proceedings in addition to ICC cases being 'triggered' by State complaints and/or referrals by the Security Council; and a recognition of the experiences of victims, particularly women and children, in armed conflict and the criminal law process.
>
> (Canadian Department of Foreign Affairs and International Trade, website)

This brief but significant list of common positions allowed many states to join the LMG while still pursuing their own policies on various more minor aspects of the Court.

Within the group, several sub-groupings could be discerned. The European Union did not visibly act as a bloc at the conference, because of the independent policy of France and, to a lesser extent, the United Kingdom, related to their permanent membership of the Security Council. However, all the other thirteen EU states were members of the LMG, many from an early stage, as were many of the accession countries. 'Europe' therefore did have a profile as part of the LMG, and according to some, its broad pro-Court stance constrained and conditioned the policies of France and the United Kingdom (Bergsmo, 1998: 347; Haq, 1998b). Since the negotiations, the European Union has taken common positions on the Court.

Another group that emerged perhaps for the first time as a powerful unity was the Southern African Development Community (SADC), consisting of fourteen states but clearly led by South Africa (Schabas,

2001: 16). This group took common positions that were in accordance with, but went beyond, those of the LMG ('Selections from Statements', 1997).

In line with Arthur Robinson's initial move towards the establishment of the Court, the member states of the Caribbean Community were strong supporters of the Court. However, they had two specific concerns, one of which was particularly at odds with the values of most civil society actors: they insisted on the inclusion of drug-related crime in the Statute, and they wished to see the death penalty included, in accordance with the domestic policy of many of these states of sentencing drugs criminals to death (Statement by Trinidad and Tobago, 1999). They were unsuccessful on both counts.

Other African and Latin American countries were not officially grouped in blocks. There was a 'Rio Group' of Latin American states, but it did not take important common positions, except against the death penalty ('Selections from Statements', 1997). Particularly in Latin America, however, virtually all states, with the exception of Mexico, were in favour of a strong, independent Court, although most of them did not officially join the LMG.

Unusually, a North–South divide was virtually absent at the ICC negotiations. The main division was between a majority of states in favour of a strong, independent Court and a minority trying to curtail its powers. While each separate sub-issue saw different divisions of states, very few of them ran along North–South lines. In the PrepComs, the Non-Aligned Movement (NAM) did play an active role, led by India and converging on two principles: no Security Council control over the Court, and inclusion of nuclear weapons in a list of prohibited weapons (Benedetti and Washburn, 1999: 31). However, a compromise proposal on the Security Council first made in 1996 was widely accepted (see Chapter 3). In Rome, NAM cohesion on nuclear weapons also broke down and, due to what Benedetti and Washburn (ibid.: 33) called 'the enthusiastic defection from the Non-Aligned Movement by sub-Saharan African states', India became increasingly isolated. As a result, the NAM, often the 'voice of the South' at these venues, had little influence (Kirsch and Holmes, 1999: 37). This absence of customary polarisations, together with the resulting defections from traditional groupings to the LMG, was one of the group's strengths.

A second strength, already mentioned, was the parsimonious list of positions LMG membership stood for. It expressed a broad feeling that the Court needed to be effective and independent, rather than being bound by the straitjacket of a complete common position on all aspects of the Statute, and allowed many states to join and yet pursue their own policies on minor issues.

The final strength of the LMG was its close association with the chair of the negotiations. The PrepComs were chaired by the Netherlands, a long-time LMG member, while Canada chaired the LMG itself. When the Dutch chair fell ill, Canada took over the chairmanship of the conference and Australia took the chair of the LMG. As a result, the chairman, Adriaan Bos and his successor, Philippe Kirsch, were able to place fellow LMG members in key 'coordinator' positions, chairing subgroups of the negotiations (Schabas, 2001: 16). Eleven of the fifteen coordinators came from members of the LMG; the crucial issues of the prosecutor, jurisdiction and admissibility were coordinated by trusted representatives of Argentina, Finland and Canada, who had each had a long involvement in the negotiations, and been long-time members of the LMG (Kirsch, 1999: 453, n. 8). This meant that these positions were in the hands of people who were strongly committed to an effective and independent Court, and who tended to recognise that global civil society actors were by and large allies in this endeavour.

By comparison with the 'friends of the Court', the states one might class as 'enemies of the Court' were much less well organised. The only exception to this were the Arab states. They took a position against the inclusion of internal armed conflicts in the subject matter for the Court. However, the 'overwhelming majority of states . . . were convinced that it would be absurd to create an ICC that had no jurisdiction over these conflicts' (Kirsch and Holmes, 1999: 9), so they were defeated. Jordan, the only 'Like-Minded' Arab state and the only state in the region to have ratified the Statute to date, deviated from the rest of the group on this issue (Haq, 1998b). The Arab group also insisted (with some civil society activists but against many others; see Chapter 5) on the deletion of the term 'gender' from the Statute, on the inclusion of the death penalty in the Statute (Schabas, 2001: 16) and on the rewording of a clause on child soldiers so as to exclude the Palestinian intifada.

The permanent members of the Security Council were initially united in the view that the Court should be subject to the control of the Security Council, as the Yugoslavia and Rwanda tribunals had been (Benedetti, 1997; Hall, 1998a: 132). After the election of a Labour government in the United Kingdom in May 1997, the United Kingdom joined the LMG. Yet it was never considered an entirely loyal and trustworthy member of the LMG. (interview Pace; see also Chapter 4). Subsequently, the French position on Security Council control also began to shift, as is discussed in further detail in Chapter 3 (Haq, 1998b).

Beyond the matter of Security Council control and nuclear weapons (see Chapter 6), the permanent five were never a coherent block (Kirsch and Holmes, 1999: 37). Russia pursued an independent policy, opposing certain parts of the draft Statute while supporting others, and ended up voting in favour of the Statute, although it has not ratified it to date. China was one of the most active opponents of the Statute, but was not taken very seriously as a negotiating partner, as it was clear that it would not consider ratifying the Statute unless it experienced an unexpected sea change in government. The most powerful opponent of the Court to have emerged since, the United States, had one of the biggest and most active delegations, which made vigorous attempts to shape the Court according to its own preferences, rather than aborting it. Its role in the negotiations is discussed extensively in the further chapters of this book.

While certain states found each other in opposition to specific proposals within the negotiations, there was no concerted effort by a group of states to scupper the negotiations altogether. Since the main enemies of the Court included China, India, Pakistan, Israel and the Arab states, it is perhaps not surprising that historic enmities within this group obstructed the growth of a 'like-minded' spirit against the Court, similar to the coalition in favour.

The NGO Coalition

A mere five or six NGOs were present at the United Nations General Assembly session in December 1994 where the ILC's draft statute was discussed. They were disappointed that instead of setting a date for a drafting conference as the ILC had recommended, the General Assembly only instituted an *ad hoc* committee to study the draft further. In particular, they had been shocked by what they considered the excessive willingness of states they considered friends of the Court to compromise (interview Pace).

A phone call between two of these observers, Bill Pace, Executive Director of the World Federalist Movement, and Chris Hall, legal adviser to Amnesty International, resulted in an invitation to a number of groups to discuss the formation of an NGO Coalition (interview Pace). On 10 February 1995, the NGO Coalition for an International Criminal Court (CICC) was founded, as 'a broad-based network of NGOs and international law experts' whose main purpose was 'to advocate the creation of an effective and just International Criminal Court' ('ABCs of the ICC', 1996). Bill Pace became the coordinator, and his organisation the World Federalist Movement, a small New

York-based group that formed part of a larger federalist network, became the secretariat. The World Federalist Movement was particularly suited to this task as the legal and human rights groups were already developing strong opinions on specific aspects of the international criminal court, and neither too much agreement nor open competition between them would have been good for the image of the Coalition. The World Federalists merely advocated the idea of an ICC in principle as part of the vision of a 'just world order through a strengthened United Nations' to which they are committed (World Federalist Movement, website). They were considered small and neutral enough to be trusted by a whole range of NGOs (interviews Pace, Dicker, Van Troost).

By the time of the Rome Conference, which took place from 15 June to 17 July 1998, the CICC had grown into a network of over 800 organisations, 236 of which sent one or more representatives to Rome. Taken collectively, the Coalition delegation was therefore far bigger than any state delegations.

The Coalition chose initially to formulate no common position except 'to advocate for the creation of an effective, just and independent International Criminal Court', and to be just a conduit of information between NGOs, state representatives and the general public, and a resource for coordination between NGOs. On the Sunday before the Rome Conference, however, the Steering Committee of the Coalition did adopt a list of 'Basic Principles' (CICC, 1998a).

Despite the loose formal structure of the CICC and the wide variety of interests of its members, it was extremely effective in its coordinating role, particularly at the Rome Conference. In order to be as effective as possible, it split up into three types of groups: regional caucuses, which lobbied state representatives of their own regions; issue-based caucuses on gender justice, victims, children, peace, and a caucus of faith-based organisations; and twelve working groups, which shadowed the working groups of state representatives on different sets of articles of the draft statute, and made daily reports available to NGOs and state delegates (Pace and Thieroff, 1999: 394).

The Latin American regional caucus consisted of sixteen NGOs, which joined forces to lobby the Latin American delegations in Rome as well as the media and parliamentarians at home. Their efforts appear to have shifted the positions of Mexico (on war crimes) and Colombia (on the inclusion of internal conflict), while Peru became a much more active proponent of the Court after an agreement was reached between NGOs and the Foreign Ministry on a number of issues (Crawford, 1998). The African and Asian Caucuses were less visible at the Conference, but the three later made joint statements as a 'tricontinental' Southern Caucus (Nel, 2002: 159).

Special themes that went across various parts of the Statute were tackled by thematic caucuses. Those concerned with children's rights, for instance, coordinated their efforts in the Children's Caucus. They 'lobbied hard', and successfully, to exempt persons under 18 from prosecution by the Court (Saland, 1999: 201; Austin, 1998). They also worked to make the use of child soldiers a war crime. In this case, the final clause was less satisfactory, prohibiting the conscription only of those under 15. States that felt that this provision did not go far enough have since developed an optional protocol raising the age to 18 for those states that ratify it (Schabas, 2001: 50; Austin, 1998). The activities of two other thematic groups, the Women's Caucus and the Weapons Systems/Peace Caucus, are discussed in detail in Chapters 5 and 6; the Faith-Based Caucus is discussed later in this chapter.

The regular reports of the twelve shadow teams were perhaps the most effective, allowing all NGOs, and the smaller state delegations, to keep abreast of all the sub-negotiations even if they could not physically be there. They also maintained close relations with the chairs of the official working group, many of whom were early promoters of the like-minded group.

Issue areas represented

Law

The establishment of an International Criminal Court can be considered as a major step towards a more accountable and people-centred international law. However, its impact on world affairs is rather more abstract and long-term than for instance the Landmines Ban Treaty or the Convention Against Torture.

It is not surprising, then, that from the beginning, the venture primarily attracted lawyers: specialists in human rights law, humanitarian law, criminal law and the law of international institutions all had a particular interest in the ICC, in which all these areas of law converged. While the initial discussions by the ILC were barely noticed or monitored by anyone, the quick transformation of the Yugoslavia tribunal from an idea into a working court excited and mobilised the legal profession. This was particularly true for young lawyers and law students: the European Law Students' Association (ELSA) had large delegations at the PrepComs and in Rome, where it had about forty students. But there were also very committed senior academics, and a few practising lawyers. Professor William Schabas, for instance, then at the University of Montreal (now at Galway), attended the whole five weeks of the Rome conference, Professor Daniel Nsereko of the University of Botswana single-handedly put the issue on the map in his country, and David Stoelting of Morgan, Lewis & Bockius raised support for the ICC at the New York Bar Association and the American Bar Association (interview Schabas; 'Regional Reports', 1997; Nsereko, 1997; Stoelting, 1997).

More than forty lawyers' associations had themselves accredited for the Rome conference, including six international associations, regional organisations like the Arab Lawyers' Union and the Latin American Institute for Alternative Legal Services (ILSA), national organisations like the Japan Federation of Bar Associations and the Association Tchadienne de Juristes (Chad Jurists' Association), local bar associations from New York and Paris, and legal NGOs like the Croatian Law Centre and the Bangladesh Legal Aid and Services Trust. These lawyers have made many contributions to the Statute, mainly on the more legal-technical issues, which are not discussed in this book. Another practising lawyer, Elise Groulx, a barrister from Montreal, took the initiative to found an International Criminal Defence Attorneys Association, to provide a pool of, and a support network for, qualified defence lawyers to plead in international criminal courts (Groulx, 1997; ICDAA website).

Human rights

Human rights organisations were particularly predominant within the campaign for an international criminal court. After decades of building an international human rights system at the regional and global levels, human rights experts began to realise that while the body of law on human rights had become substantial, the scale of human rights violations in the world was not actually declining. The emphasis therefore shifted towards implementation. In this new thinking, it became increasingly clear that thinking of human rights violations as perpetrated by monolithic and abstract entities called states, and holding only states responsible, obscured the complexities of internal and external power structures, and stood in the way of human rights enforcement. The emphasis shifted towards punishing individual perpetrators. The term 'impunity' begins to crop up in the reports of human rights organisations in the early 1990s (Goldman, 1989; Lutz, 1990; LCHR, 1991; AI, 1991), and shortly afterwards in the academic literature. The experience in many Latin American and other countries after transition to democracy was that it was not just legally, but also politically, socially and psychologically, very difficult to prosecute former perpetrators of human rights violations (see, for instance, Artucio, 1992a, b; Roht-Arriaza, 1995; Sieder, 1995).

Thus, the idea of taking recourse to an international criminal court came to be embraced by human rights groups. However, the Nuremberg and Tokyo tribunals, and to a lesser extent the Yugoslavia and Rwanda tribunals, were seen as selective and lacking in impartiality, as they had been set up by a few states, to prosecute only in a few circumscribed situations. The ICC would be set up by the international community, and have a global remit.

Amazingly, there was no tradition in international human rights law of assigning criminal responsibility to individual perpetrators of violations. Building such rules from existing legal principles was the intellectual and political challenge of the ICC. However, establishing a criminal court rather than just holding states accountable required some adjustments of thought. The focus of human rights advocates with respect to criminal trials had always instinctively been on safeguarding the rights of the defendant. Now, the rights of suspects – in effect enemies of human rights – the rights of victims and the interest in creating an effective system capable of convicting perpetrators had to be balanced against each other.

While the idea of 'combating impunity' was developed primarily in Latin America, the first experiences with international criminal justice came from South-East Europe and Central Africa, where the tribunals were just beginning their work. Interest from human rights organisations in the ICC was truly worldwide, including regional organisations such as the InterAfrican Union for Human Rights, many national organisations such as Australian Lawyers for Human Rights, the Comisión Chilena de Derechos Humanos (Chilean Human Rights Commission) or the Human Rights Commission of Pakistan, local organisations like Minnesota Advocates for Human Rights and more specialised organisations such as the European Roma Rights Centre and Redress, which seeks reparation for survivors of torture.

However, the large international human rights organisations were very dominant. They all had full-time staff almost entirely devoted to the ICC, they wrote most of the advocacy documents relating to the Court, and the CICC's Steering Committee consisted almost exclusively of these groups, including Amnesty International, Human Rights Watch, the Lawyers Committee for Human Rights, the Fédération Internationale des Ligues de Droits de l'Homme (International

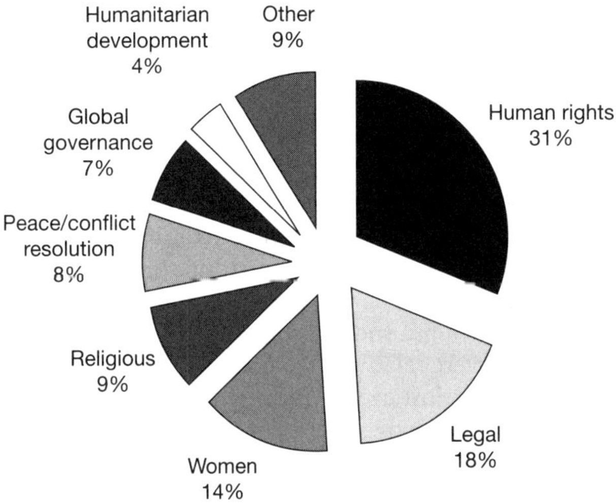

Figure 2.1 NGOs accredited to the Rome negotiations: functional representation.

Federation for Human Rights) and the International Commission of Jurists. The problems raised by this dominance are discussed in later chapters, particularly Chapters 6 and 7.

Gender

Women's groups were also particularly inspired by the example of the Yugoslavia tribunal in their work for an international criminal court. While others had pointed out before that women were particularly vulnerable to abuse in conflicts, attention drawn to the use of rape as a component of ethnic cleansing in the former Yugoslavia brought the issue to the fore (Steains, 1999: 359). Although the statute of the Yugoslavia tribunal did not contain any gender-specific mandate, its functionaries recognised that an ostensibly gender-neutral justice system would in fact fail to address gender-specific abuses, and took on board some of the concerns of women's groups. An officer for gender issues was appointed within the prosecutor's office, and it was decided to allow rape victims to give testimony anonymously, and to seriously prosecute rape as a war crime, an issue to which the first prosecutor, Richard Goldstone, was particularly committed (Sharratt and Kaschak, 1999: 12–13, 31, 54). It was in their relations with the tribunal in The Hague that Yugoslavian women and their international supporters had their first experience of enscribing women's concerns into humanitarian law, an experience they built on in New York and Rome (Durham, 2000a).

Other important experiences included the World Conference on Human Rights in Vienna in 1993 and the Fourth World Conference on Women in Beijing in 1995 (Steains, 1999: 360; Facio, 1998: 1). These were not treaty-making conferences, however, and the challenge for women's rights groups was to take the progressive texts of these 'aspirational' final declarations into the 'mainstream big-boy venue of hard-core international law' of the ICC negotiations (interview Hall Martinez).

While some women's groups, such as Equality Now, had been involved since 1995, most were relative latecomers to the process. The Women's Caucus for Gender Justice was formed at the initiative of a small group of women's rights activists present at the February 1997 PrepCom, who realised that without a much stronger effort, gender concerns were not going to be adequately represented in the negotiations. It quickly grew to be a coalition within a coalition, with more than 300 member organisations by the time of the Rome conference (Facio, 1998: 1–3).

Anti-abortion and pro-family concerns

As in Beijing and other fora, the feminist majority of women's groups in New York and Rome, focused on women's rights, met a vocal minority of anti-abortion groups, supported by the Vatican and Arab states, whose preoccupation was to prevent any language that might be interpreted as facilitating abortion from entering the Statute (interviews Hall Martinez and Pace; REAL Women, 1998a, b).

While abortion was their primary concern, their agenda was wider, including concerns about 'forced social change by feminist, homosexual and other radical groups' (Campaign Life Coalition quoted in 'ICC: Promise of Justice or Threat of Tyranny?', 1998). They came to the negotiations in order to oppose what they saw as dangerous proposals by the Women's Caucus, but they did not so much strive for a Statute that would reflect their concerns, as oppose the agreement of a Statute and establishment of a Court generally, as 'many pro-lifers also see the court as a crucial step in the abandonment of national sovereignty, and the establishment of a tyrannical world government' ('ICC: Promise of Justice or Threat of Tyranny?', 1998). These groups and their views posed quite a challenge to the other civil society groups and individuals, who were all pro-Court in one way or another. The dispute between the women's groups and the pro-family groups, the relations both had with other civil society actors and with states, and the implications of this conflict for theorisation of the role of global civil society in international law-making are all dealt with in Chapter 5.

Peace and conflict resolution

The aims of the smaller peace contingent within the movement for an ICC were less clear. There were three kinds of peace groups. Organisations such as the academically minded German Development and Peace Foundation, the Spanish Movimiento por la Paz, el Desarme y la Libertad and the Indian Institute for Peace, Disarmament and Environment Protection have very broad aims, including furthering sustainable development and protecting the environment as well as different peace, disarmament and conflict resolution concerns.

The second, typified for instance by the Nuclear Age Peace Foundation and the International Association of Lawyers against Nuclear Arms, were direct descendants of the nuclear disarmament movement of the 1980s, and their primary interest in the proposed international criminal court was to have the threat or use of nuclear arms characterised as a war crime. The organisations of this type represented in Rome were predominantly from the United States. As is discussed in Chapter 6, they were largely unsuccessful.

The third, characterised by national NGOs such as the Colombian Observatorio de la Paz (Peace Observatory), international NGOs like International Alert, and networks like the Helsinki Citizens' Assembly and the Pan-African Reconciliation Centre partly had roots in the same movement, but have evolved in a different direction through direct involvement in the non-nuclear conflicts of the 1990s, in which abuse of civilians became a primary method of warfare. They were exploring solutions in the direction of grassroots conflict resolution on the one hand, and a more human-rights-based approach on the other (Kaldor, 2001: 113–117). Their interests in the Court were much more similar to those of the human rights groups than to those of the anti-nuclear groups (interview Pace).

Global governance

A small but very active contingent of groups could be characterised as 'global governance' organisations, committed generally to promoting a more just and more democratic global order. This included various world federalist organisations as well as local UN associations, both of which propagate the idea of a strong United Nations, as well as following the actual organisation critically. It was one of these, the World Federalist Movement, which became the coordinator and secretariat of the CICC.

Three other organisations, which belong to neither the federalist nor the UN associations category, were particularly actively involved in the campaign for an international criminal court. The Italian organisation No Peace Without Justice was founded in 1993 in response to the atrocities in Yugoslavia, and campaigns primarily for an effective system of justice through international tribunals. Parliamentarians for Global Action is a peculiar organisation that stretches the boundaries of what is commonly understood as civil society: it is an international NGO whose members consist of national parliamentarians. Also stretching the boundaries, and in a category all by itself, there is the International Committee of the Red Cross. It has a special position, more exalted than that of ordinary non-governmental organisations, in negotiations that fall within the remit of international humanitarian law, having stood at the cradle of the Geneva (or Red Cross) Conventions, and being the only organisation explicitly designated in those conventions to carry out humanitarian tasks such as tending the wounded and visiting prisoners of war. In the ICC negotiations, which concerned a hybrid of humanitarian concerns, human rights, criminal and institutional law, they were less dominant, but were still regularly invited to address the plenary session of states (see also Chapter 6).

Religion

Finally, a number of religious groups and churches were represented. The Christian universe dominated, with mainstream denominations like the Lutheran World Federation, the Friends (Quakers) and the United Methodists, religious orders such as the Franciscans, and faith-based NGOs such as the Catholic Commission for Justice and Peace in Zimbabwe, the Fédération Internationale des Chrétiens pour l'Abolition de la Torture (International Christians' Federation for the Abolition of Torture) and the Fundación Ecuménica para el Desarrollo y la Paz (Ecumenical Peace and Development Foundation). Jews and Muslims were also represented at a high level, with the participation of the Coordinating Board of Jewish Organizations and the World Muslim Congress. The Buddhist Lama Gangchen World Peace Foundation and the Bahai International Community, which is often active at human rights venues, were also represented. Most of these groups united themselves in a Faith-Based Caucus (Faith-Based Caucus, 1997).

The Faith-Based Caucus represented an emerging consensus among religious groups at the end of the twentieth century – 'the century that has seen the killing of more humans by other humans than occurred in all the rest of our history put together' (Shriver, 1997) – around the need for more earthly justice, to place besides eternal, divine justice. Their aim was, however, to go beyond mere punishment, from punitive justice to restorative justice, to help reconcile communities torn by violence, and to inject a spiritual dimension into the ICC project (Faith-Based Caucus, 1997).

The Faith-Based Caucus particularly concerned itself with the less political, more ethically oriented preamble of the Statute: having found that the brief and prosaic January 1998 draft did 'not as yet have a clear and inspiring vision', it submitted its own draft preamble (Faith-Based Caucus, 1998). While the subsequent preamble was in fact drafted on the basis of a number of state proposals (Clark and Slade, 1999: 425–429), it may indeed have been the Caucus which spurred it to employ a more 'inspiring and visionary discourse' (Faith-Based Caucus, 1998). According to members of the Samoan delegation, which coordinated the negotiations on the preamble, '[m]ost of the concepts the Faith-Based Caucus espoused can be found in the final product, albeit in different language' (Clark and Slade, 1999: 425).

Geographical representation

When the Coalition for an International Criminal Court was founded in 1995, it consisted primarily of international NGOs, usually with European or American headquarters, and a permanent representation at the United Nations in New York. However, a strong effort was made to involve national organisations from all regions in the coalition, and not without success. As explained earlier, Latin American organisations had a strong interest in the Court stemming from their own experience of living through dictatorships, and the subsequent difficulties in bringing perpetrators of violations to justice. Indeed, most of the Latin American organisations involved were human rights organisations (sometimes church based).

African organisations, mainly lawyers' and human rights groups, also apparently believed in the international criminal court as part of a 'rule of law' solution to the wars and human rights abuses many of their countries had experienced. Their interest may also have been fuelled by the active involvement of African lawyers like the Senegalese Abdul Koroma, one of the most active members of the International Law Commission's sub-commission on the ICC (Krieger, 1998), the

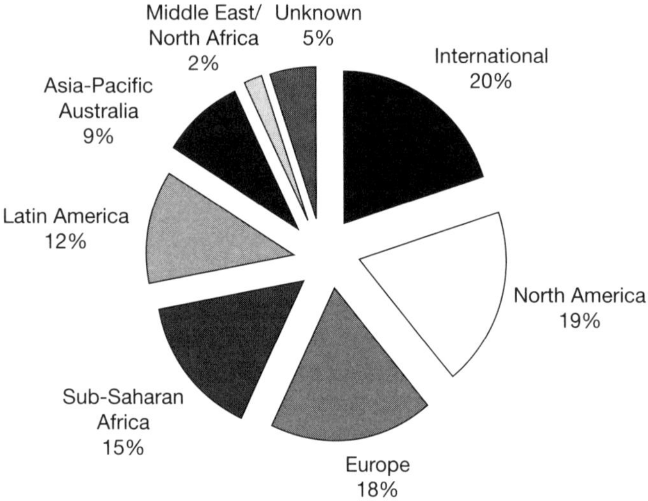

Figure 2.2 NGOs accredited to the Rome negotiations: regional representation.

South African Richard Goldstone, prosecutor of the Yugoslavia tribunal, and by the setting up of the Rwanda tribunal, in which the South African judge Navi Pillay came to play a pivotal role.

While a wide range of East and West European and North American organisations were also well represented, there were relatively fewer groups from Asia. Representation from the Middle East and North Africa was even weaker, with just five groups accredited to the Rome conference.

While unfortunate, this lack of interest is not difficult to understand. It is not so much, as is sometimes claimed by Northern groups when it comes to Southern representation in global fora, that they were 'too busy with their own issues'. That, after all, could have been at least equally true for the Africans and Latin Americans. A more important factor is that what was being set up in Rome was not a court that was to be imposed on the world, but a consensual agreement. While universal jurisdiction was considered (see Chapter 4), it was most likely that states would first have to ratify the Statute before being bound by it. A quick glance at ratification of existing human rights treaties, for instance the International Covenant on Civil and Political Rights or the Convention against Torture, shows that, regardless of their official ideology, states from these two regions are least likely to become parties to international treaties.

It is not surprising, then, that the enthusiasm of civil society groups from these regions for setting up an even more forceful human rights implementation mechanism, one that their governments would be even less likely to participate in, would be lukewarm. However, there were some groups represented in Rome, and an Asian Network for the International Criminal Court (ANICC) has since been founded, with particularly active chapters in Bangladesh, Thailand and the Philippines. At the time of writing, official support from the Asian region still lags well behind other regions, with just twelve ratifications, half of which are from very small states.

At the time of writing, only one country from the Middle East and North Africa region, Jordan, has ratified the ICC treaty. However, civil society groups in the region have begun to take up the issue more enthusiastically, organising regional workshops in Egypt, Jordan and, most recently and most ambitiously, in Yemen in January 2004. While they are well aware that ratification by the governments of the region may be far off, their approach now is to first spread information about and build support for the ICC in the realm of civil society, in the hope that governments may one day follow (Manaá, 2003, personal communication).

Methods and forms of action

Lobbying

The lobbying of state representatives was undoubtedly the most important activity for nearly all global civil society actors that took an interest in the ICC. While lobbying efforts were to some extent coordinated by the NGO Coalition for an International Criminal Court, there was not a single, consolidated campaign. Each group, and many individuals, pursued their own interests and strategies.

Lobbying took place at the official PrepComs and in Rome, of course, but also in a wide range of other fora. Organisations sought meetings with officials of their national Justice, Foreign Affairs and Defence departments, trying to awaken interest in and support for the Court. They were always a presence at intergovernmental conferences, such as the American Heads of State summit in Santiago de Chile in April 1998. Many of these intergovernmental conferences, such as the Southern African Development Cooperation meeting of Justice Ministers in South Africa in September 1997, a pan-African conference in Dakar in February 1998 and a Caribbean conference in Trinidad in May 1998, were in fact co-organised by governments and NGOs

(Lifton and Norris, 1997; 'Governments and Civil Society Meet', 1998; Gonzalez Cueva, 1998).

Another very important forum for NGO lobbying was the informal meetings at Cherif Bassiouni's International Institute for the Higher Criminal Sciences in Siracusa, Sicily. At these meetings, which took place in between PrepCom sessions, a select group of NGO representatives as well as mainly 'pro-court' state representatives were invited to discuss and thrash out further details of the future Court. According to a Dutch diplomat, these meetings

> were extremely instrumental. No difference was made there between state delegates and NGOs, we were all there as experts. It was very informal, there was lots of sunshine, good food, that had an impact on the negotiations, there was more space, we had fun, it was pleasant, relaxed. It was an instrument for taking further steps.
>
> (interview Von Hebel)

The lobbying of state representatives was the main purpose of most organisations in coming to Rome, as evidenced by the fact that, quite unusually, there was no separate NGO forum to the conference. Conference lobbying and domestic lobbying were coordinated; according to CICC coordinator Bill Pace,

> When national delegations or portions thereof (e.g. specific ministries) needed reinforcement, or when concerns arose that a delegation might be compromising key principles, the Coalition contacted ministers, parliamentarians and media in the capital through its national networks. This type of conference-to-capital coordination has been a goal of NGOs at many conferences; for many of us its effective implementation in Rome was a first.
>
> (Pace and Thieroff, 1999: 395)

Producing expert documents

At the same time, a great deal of specialist documentation was produced by individuals and organisations involved in the ICC process. This took two main forms: journal articles, especially in legal journals, by individuals (sometimes written by the staff of NGOs, such as Christopher Hall of Amnesty, but more often by academics); and reports by NGOs. Both had the primary aim of informing and influencing a specialist public of NGOs, academics and state representatives on specific sub-themes, promoting certain alternatives over others with reference to precedent, legal argument or political realities (see Lyonette, website for an extensive bibliography of the ICC). According to the Dutch delegation leader, Theo Van Boven, who came late to the process to replace his sick colleague,

> [T]he papers of the four or five bigger organisations – Amnesty, Human Rights Watch, International Service for Human Rights, the Lawyers Committee for Human Rights, the International Commission of Jurists – have been extremely helpful to me; that was real quality input. They were very good, and they made an impact.
>
> (interview Van Boven)

Convening conferences

One of the most prevalent forms of action in the years leading up to the Rome conference was the organisation of national and international conferences, expert meetings, public debates, seminars, symposia, and workshops. Such meetings were organised all over Europe, in Southern and West Africa, South Asia, North, South and Central America and the Caribbean.

There was less activity elsewhere in Asia and in North Africa and the Middle East, which is in line with the figures on civil society participation from these regions in Rome. Indeed, in many of these countries there is no tradition of government tolerance for public debates about the country's foreign policy.

The conferences were often either organised by NGOs or academic institutions, or co-organised between these and the national governments. They were characterised by an intermingling of officials with the NGO and the activist communities, and by high-level legal debates, rather than political confrontations. Some were regional or international in character, but even the national meetings often boasted one or more international guests drawn from the ranks of the NGO Coalition, the Yugoslavia and Rwanda tribunals, or from the academic community.

Thus, a global specialist debate about the international criminal court, involving academics, NGO advocates, practising lawyers and state officials, was going on in the years leading up to the Rome conference, through the numerous expert conferences, the Siracusa retreats, and the law journals and NGO publications, as well as in the official PrepCom meetings.

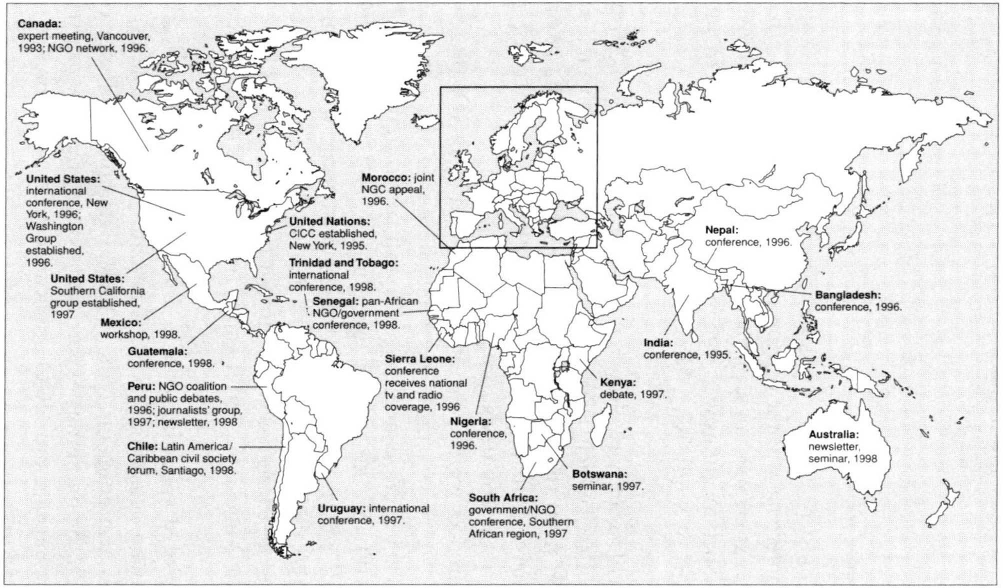

European action on the International Criminal Court

Austria: international conference, 1998.

Denmark: international conference, 1997.

EU: European Parliament Declaration, Brussels, 1996; Symposium at EP, Brussels, 1997.

France: NGO coalition formed, 1997.

Greece: petition, 1997.

Iceland: conference, 1996.

Italy: expert conferences, Sicily 1990, 1995, 1996, 1997; conference, Turin, 1996; NGO coalition formed, 1997; human carpet manifestation, Rome, 1998.

The Netherlands: CICC press conference, 1996.

Norway: seminar for East/Central European NGOs, Oslo, 1998.

Poland: seminar, 1998; network, 1998.

Portugal: coalition, 1998.

Russia: appeal for ICC sent to government, 1998; seminar, 1998

Spain: NGO press conference, 1998

Switzerland: conference, 1998.

Ukraine: collection of signatures in main square, Kiev, 1997.

United Kingdom: international conference, 1997; coalition formed, 1997.

Map 2.1 Global action on the International Criminal Court, 1993–1998.

Dissemination to a wider audience

While most of these meetings, and the longer NGO reports and law journal articles on the ICC, were aimed at an already informed specialist audience, the idea of an international criminal court was also disseminated to a much wider public. A strong effort was made by organisations at the national and sometimes even local level to attract the attention and support of the press for the international criminal court. The general aims of the court, and its consequences for the country in question, were explained at press conferences and by putting together media kits. Big-name international lawyers guest-authored articles, even in local newspapers, particularly in the United States (see, for instance, Bassiouni, 1996; Nanda, 1996). Intermediate between the mass media and specialist publications were dedicated newsletters, as published in Australia and Peru, and, on the international level, the Coalition's own *ICC Monitor*, which keeps interested audiences abreast of the developments in articles that avoided or explained specialist legal jargon (*ICC Monitor* website).

Big-membership organisations such as Amnesty International and the World Federalist Movement, and some of the churches, including the Friends and the Mennonites, disseminated the ideas behind the court to their own millions of members. Other organisations gathered signatures from celebrities including the Dalai Lama, Queen Noor of Jordan, Jean-Bertrand Aristide of Haiti and the former US President Jimmy Carter in favour of the court, and published these in an appeal in the *International Herald Tribune* and *Le Monde* (Busdachin, 1997).

At the Rome conference, no fewer than three daily news teams set up camp. The Coalition transformed its two-monthly *Monitor* into a daily newsletter, the InterPress Service published a series of its *Terra Viva* newspaper, as it does at all major UN conferences, and the Advocacy Project, an NGO that specialises in activist newsletters, produced *On the Record*, which was also e-mailed to about four thousand subscribers (*On the Record*, website; *Terra Viva*, website).

According to chairman Kirsch and his deputy,

> As the conference developed, so did the interest of delegates in *Terra Viva*. They read about recent events in which they had not personally participated, and also read comments about their own activities and positions. *Terra Viva* had its share of inaccuracies, but it was generally well written, well informed, and provocative enough to ensure wide readership.
>
> (Kirsch and Holmes, 1999: 11)

According to another participant, 'numerous delegations awaited with interest and enthusiasm the "new highlights" from these news sources' (Almeida 1999: 15).

Seeking and use of funding

The NGO Coalition and its constituent organisations needed, of course, to raise funds for their activities to support the establishment of the court. Initially, the World Federalist Movement went tens of thousands of dollars into debt, and relied largely on volunteer labour by graduate students in setting up the Coalition. Later, the Ford Foundation, the MacArthur Foundation and the European Union, as well as some governments, made grants both to the Coalition and to many of its constituent organisations (interview Pace). The money thus raised was particularly used to bring more Southern NGOs and academic experts to New York and Rome, and to prepare and disseminate campaign material (Facio, 1998: 2, 4; interviews Pace, Donat-Cattin, Hall Martinez).

The participation of other relevant experts was also made possible by funding channelled through civil society: thus, the presence of high-level officials from the Yugoslavia and Rwanda tribunals at the negotiations was made possible by an external grant applied for by the Coalition (interview Pace).

The coordination, research and lobbying efforts of the Coalition and its members were primarily self-funded, however, through member donations, through the use of volunteers, including many students and academics, and by finding ways of allocating staff and resources from other departments and projects towards the ICC (interviews Pace, Donat-Cattin, Dicker, Hall Martinez, Burroughs).

Provision of experts and interns

Another type of activity that supported the process of negotiations, and particularly the fuller participation of Southern governments in the process, was the provision of legal experts and interns from civil society to the state delegations. This allowed them to be present at more parallel meetings, as well as helping to develop their legal arguments. Some governments, including those of Canada and Costa Rica, included NGO representatives in their delegations as a gesture of goodwill. Others, including Bosnia, Trinidad and Tobago, Sierra Leone, Senegal, Burundi and Congo, relied on a technical assistance programme by No Peace Without Justice to augment the size and expertise of their delegations. Other countries engaged the services of domestic (Germany, the Netherlands and the United States) or foreign (Samoa, the Solomon Islands) professors of law as delegation members. According to one source, 'public and private experts' were the largest element in the state delegations, outnumbering career diplomats and senior civil servants (Benedetti and Washburn, 1999: 16). Needless to say, this kind of expertise would not be entirely neutral and malleable to government positions. These 'experts-on-loan' came with independent views, and influenced the delegations from within.

Andrew Clapham, the lawyer engaged by the Solomon Islands, for instance, sought, ultimately without success, to make it possible to indict not just individuals before the court, but also companies (Saland, 1999: 199). This was not a task foisted on him by his employer: it was an issue in which he had a strong personal interest, and on which he has published since – he is now a special adviser to the High Commissioner on Human Rights on corporate responsibility (Clapham web page).

Street action

Finally, some direct actions were organised in relation to the ICC. Amnesty International and No Peace Without Justice were two organisations that took many actions aimed at drawing the attention of the general public. Amnesty's Croatian section organised a demonstration in 1996, and its Ukrainian section collected signatures in Kiev's main square (Wolf, 1997). In Rome, Amnesty International organised an open-air demonstration, a 'human carpet' to represent the victims of genocide, war crimes and crimes against humanity on 4 July, and No Peace Without Justice undertook a twenty-four-hour vigil outside the Food and Agriculture Organization (FAO) building on the 16th, waiting to celebrate or mourn the final outcome of the conference ('NGO Activities', 1998). There were also some more confrontational demonstrations. During the first week in Rome, the Mothers of the Plaza de Mayo sneaked into the plenary hall, unfolded a banner reminding the delegates of the unresolved plight of Argentina's 30,000 'disappeared' political prisoners and disrupted the speech of the Argentinian justice minister. Eventually, they were forcibly led away by FAO uniformed guards, drawing much media attention ('Madres Thrown Out', 1998). A few weeks later (and a day after a delegate had 'complained' to the newspaper *Terra Viva* about the lack of demonstrations), fifty members of the Zapatista solidarity group Ya Basta demonstrated just outside the FAO building on Friday at noon, demanding that Mexico's President Ernesto Zedillo be the first person to be indicted by the ICC for 'genocide against the Mayan people' ('Indict Zedillo First', 1998). It is not clear whether they really believed such an indictment to be possible; more likely, they used the occasion to publicise their case. Such actions were few and far between, however: for every demonstration, there were dozens of conferences on the ICC.

CICC–LMG relations

Relations between the successive (LMG) chairs of the state negotiations and the coordinator of the CICC were very cordial. According to the first chair,

> NGOs have a useful function: they can add a dimension, even though such organisations are often focused on one issue. I was delighted with the way the Coalition succeeded in making all the NGO interests into a coherent unity, as I saw the importance of involving them, but I could not consult with every individual NGO.
>
> (interview Bos; translation mine)

The later chair, Kirsch, has written that NGOs 'provided substantial expert advice to virtually all delegations on the full range of complex legal issues contained in the statute' and 'served to remind delegations, on a daily basis, that the issues before the conference were very real and required urgent and effective action' (Kirsch and Holmes, 1999: 37).

The coordinators of the working groups, mainly drawn from the Like-Minded Group, also tended to have good relations with their counterparts in the shadow teams. They were contact points for the lobbying efforts of the NGOs as well as sources of information about the crucial 'informal sessions', which by and large were closed to NGOs. According to Richard Dicker of Human Rights Watch,

> [T]here were certainly times that we got particularly good accounts of the substantive debates, of who were the big players in the informal. Particularly in Rome it is safe to say that we got those, as the stakes were so high, and our contribution was valued.
>
> (interview Dicker)

The level of recognition of the Coalition's role by state representatives and United Nations officials was unprecedented. Before the

Rome conference, the Coalition's coordinator was actually asked by the United Nations to organise the accreditation of NGOs to the conference, a unique form of self-regulation not attempted before at international conferences (Pace, 1999: 209). He decided to accept the mandate because 'the UN was at the height of its financial crisis, the legal office had never done accreditation before, and I thought if I would turn down the request it would result in tremendous restraints'. However, while it was an indication of the trust placed in the CICC coordinator by the chair of the negotiations and the responsible UN official, Pace does not recommend the practice for the future, describing it as 'excruciating' and 'a design for disaster' (interview Pace). He decided to interpret his mandate as encouraging the widest possible participation, and 'only turned down one or two GONGOs [government-organised NGOs]' (interview Pace). According to two civil society participants, 'the CICC and its members achieved full legitimacy and great, sometimes determinative, influence as brokers of solutions to impasses, as experts, and even as confidants' (Benedetti and Washburn, 1999: 25). How did this come about?

In terms of militancy and visibility, the style of the ICC campaign stands in marked contrast to more recent movements, such as the anti-capitalist protests in Seattle, Genoa and many other places, or the movement that emerged against the war in Iraq. As Benedetti and Washburn (1999: 25) write, 'NGOs . . . had learned to accept a great deal in the institutional culture and style of international treaty conferences, which many of them had previously inclined to ignore. This included matters of procedure, timing, access to documents, decorum, and even dress.' If these people were representing the 'wretched of the earth', they certainly did so in less dramatic fashion than those bashing at the gates in Seattle and Genoa.

Moreover, the lines between civil society and state officials were not very sharp ones. The negotiations for an ICC were marked by a good deal of cross-over between academics, NGO staff and state representatives.

State representatives or diplomats are usually conceptualised in international relations theory as empty vessels, neutral implementers of whatever policies their employers devise. In reality, they do of course have opinions, beliefs, even feelings, on the subjects they negotiate. According to Benedetti and Washburn, 'Most of those participating in the PrepCom had the same essential and emphatic feelings, thoughts, and beliefs about war crimes, genocide, and crimes against humanity' (1999: 25). Moreover, while many state delegates had still expressed open opposition to the Court in the ad hoc committee, 'none were willing to say in the PrepCom that they opposed the Court' (ibid.: 20). This widely shared belief in the values behind the Court, and the fact that openly challenging the benefits of the Court *per se* became increasingly taboo, formed a point of leverage for global civil society.

While there clearly was a constructive relationship between LMG and CICC, the two sides saw the relationship in a different light. The Dutch chair, Adriaan Bos, called the aims of the NGOs and the LMG 'completely parallel' (interview Bos). His successor, Philippe Kirsch, also saw the relationship in an instrumental light: 'The advice provided by the NGOs contributed significantly to the comprehension and, therefore, to the acceptance of the statute by states, especially those with small delegations in Rome' (Kirsch and Holmes, 1999: 36). But CICC coordinator Bill Pace made 'the caveat that some like-minded group delegates were willing to achieve much less, NGOs pressed for greater specificity and strength. . . . We were constantly upping the ante, rather than that the NGOs were supported by the LMG' (interview Pace). Richard Dicker of Human Rights Watch, too, perceived the role of the CICC as 'stiffening the resolve' and 'fortifying the better instincts' of states (interview Dicker). Throughout 1997, for instance, the CICC 'pressed the Like-Minded Group of Countries to identify key principles which would guide the bloc in negotiations' (Pace, 1999: 206; see also Benedetti and Washburn, 1999: 23).

On one level, many participants felt like a single community in pursuit of a common goal, but on another level they were aware of the different missions of civil society and states. While civil society actors placed much emphasis on informing and persuading state representatives, they devoted attention to informing a wider public as well, and, while their relations with state delegates were mostly cordial, they did not hesitate to expose and condemn official behaviour they did not like.

There was a creative tension, therefore, sometimes glossed over but also exploited by the Coalition and many of its members, between the idea of a single community working towards a common goal, and the idea of civil society activists and state representatives as separate and sometimes antagonistic communities.

3 The victory

The independent prosecutor

This chapter and the next discuss the negotiations on the rules that determine under what circumstances a case can be tried by the International Criminal Court. Four interrelated issues were at stake here: the division of competencies between national courts and the ICC; the way in which a case could come to the attention of the Court; which parties, if any, might block a case from being heard by the Court; and the extent of the jurisdiction of the Court.

The first of these issues took up much negotiation time in the PrepComs, but much less in Rome. The general principle that was agreed early on was that of 'complementarity': the ICC was to be only complementary to national courts, and would act only if national courts were 'unwilling or unable' to deal with a case. This of course left unresolved the hot issue of who was to determine whether a state was 'unwilling or unable'. One possible avenue was to develop objective criteria: a state might, for instance, take a case back from the ICC by instituting its own prosecution. This would still leave the way open for sham proceedings aimed at shielding suspects from ICC prosecution, however. The other possibility was to give the judges of the ICC the authority to decide whether or not a state was 'willing and able', and whether, therefore, ICC proceedings were needed. This solution was agreed upon in the August 1997 PrepCom (Hall, 1998a: 130–131), to the satisfaction of a number of NGOs (Broomhall, 1998: 14–15). In March 1998, the United States proposed to add to this a provision giving states an early opportunity to challenge the Court's jurisdiction, which was indeed added (Kirsch and Holmes, 1999: 19). During the Rome conference, Mexico made an attempt to reopen the discussion on the text of the article ('Movement on Admissibility', 1998), but this met with little support, and the provision was adopted as Article 17 of the Statute, on admissibility, without major controversy.

While complementarity was one strand in the whole Gordian knot of negotiations on how the Court would come by its cases, it was a minor, relatively uncomplicated strand, and it received less attention than the others. It is not discussed in further detail in this book. The other three strands are discussed in two separate chapters. This chapter deals with the ways in which cases would come to the attention of the Court, which came to be known as 'trigger mechanisms', and possible blocks on these triggers by the Security Council. The next chapter discusses jurisdiction. In reality, however, these negotiations were intertwined: those states that sought a restrictive role for the Court and those that advocated an effective, active and independent Court both worked on several fronts simultaneously. For the former, constraining the powers of the Court in one of these areas would be enough to achieve their aims, whereas the latter needed success on all fronts to achieve their overall aim.

International Law Commission draft

The 1994 draft by the ILC listed only two ways in which an investigation could be initiated, or 'triggered', as it came to be called. States parties could lodge a complaint alleging that a crime had been committed, or the UN Security Council could refer a matter to the Court. Unlike in domestic criminal law systems, the ICC's prosecutor could not institute any investigations him- or herself. Moreover, if the Security Council was dealing with a related situation as a breach of or threat to peace, no prosecution could go ahead without permission from the Security Council, which meant that each of its permanent members had a veto on prosecutions (ILC, 1997: art. 23, 25).

With hindsight, it seems difficult to understand why the ILC, which was an independent body not supposed to be influenced by the political considerations of states, took such a restrictive approach to the initiation of proceedings. Only one member suggested that the prosecutor might take up cases in the absence of a complaint, but the others deemed this inappropriate 'at the present stage of development of the international legal system' (Fernández de Gurmendi, 1999: 175). One young lawyer involved in the ICC campaign commented that 'some professors of law are more conservative than the worst diplomats' (interview Donat-Cattin). Be this as it may, the ILC's sense of the stage of development of international law was probably accurate at the time it wrote its draft. As is shown in what follows, however, state views on the matter evolved rapidly in the next few years.

Ad Hoc Committee

Amnesty International, which produced one of the earliest NGO documents on the ICC, recommended that 'the Prosecutor should be able to initiate investigations on his or her own initiative or after receiving a complaint by or on behalf of an individual', arguing that the ILC draft had envisaged the Court as 'a tool for states parties, rather than a tool for the general public' (AI, 1994: 27). However, this recommendation was hidden away in the main text of a long report. It was not one of Amnesty's key recommendations at this time, perhaps suggesting that it was not considered achievable by the organisation. Another early document, by the International Commission of Jurists (ICJ), did not suggest that the prosecutor should act on his or her own initiative, but rather that complaints from victims should be able to initiate proceedings (ICJ, 1995: section 5C).

Amnesty International pointed out that complaints by states or by the Security Council might be politicised; both organisations expressed concern that very few cases would be likely to come to the Court. The Amnesty report argued that existing state complaint procedures under human rights treaties are very rarely used, while the ICJ demonstrated that there are various precedents in human rights treaties for acting on individual complaints. Amnesty International also opposed the Security Council's ability to prevent investigations and prosecutions (AI, 1994: 21).

In August 1995, some states, including Austria, Greece, the Netherlands, Norway and Switzerland, began to voice the idea of a prosecutor initiating proceedings on his or her own. They did so in very cautious terms, saying for instance that the prosecutor's role was 'too narrow' and needed to be 'more active', and that 'possible enhancement of the prosecutor's role needed further examination' (UN, 1995c). At the same time, a much smaller number of states, including Chile and the Czech Republic, made the further-reaching suggestion that individuals, victims and/or NGOs should be able to trigger a procedure (UN, 1995a, b). Most states did not yet take a position on trigger mechanisms at this early stage, when it was still very uncertain whether there would be a court at all. The United States, however, was already making it clear in the General Assembly in November 1995 that in its view, only the Security Council should be allowed to refer cases.

PrepComs

At the first PrepCom meeting in April 1996, Amnesty International representative Christopher Hall observed that a 'significantly larger group of delegations than in the Ad Hoc Committee argued that the prosecutor should have the power to initiate investigations ex officio or on the basis of information obtained from any source' (Hall, 1997a: 182). However, a UN press release still stated that 'Speakers were almost unanimous in opposing the granting of powers to the prosecutor of the court to initiate an investigation on his own, based on information received, without the consent of the States concerned' (UN, 1996). Nonetheless, the option of a prosecutor with *ex officio* (by virtue of his or her office) or *proprio motu* (on his or her own initiative) authority to initiate prosecutions, also referred to simply as an 'independent prosecutor', was added to the draft Statute in brackets.

During 1996, more NGOs began to publish documents commenting on the Statute, and they all insisted on the right of the prosecutor to start prosecutions either on his or her own initiative, or on the basis of victim and NGO complaints (HRW, 1996; LCHR, 1996; ELSA, 1996; Pax Romana, 1996). In 1997, further voices were added to the chorus (IPB, 1997; WC, 1997a; FIDH, 1997: Stoelting, 1997). Gradually, the independence of the prosecutor became the single biggest issue on the agenda of the CICC and many of its constituent organisations. An Amnesty International representative called it a 'collective bottom line' (interview Van Troost).

In August 1997, in order to overcome the objections of those who opposed an independent prosecutor, Argentina informally proposed that the prosecutor might be allowed to pursue his or her own investigations, subject to the permission of a pre-trial chamber of judges. However, the 'proposal insufficiently addressed the concerns of some States regarding the need to prevent a politically motivated or frivolous decision of the Prosecutor being launched' (Fernández de Gurmendi, 1999: 183). In this session, Christopher Hall reported again that an 'increasing number of states supported giving the prosecutor the power to initiate investigations on his or her own motion', but equally, 'a large number of states, including all five permanent members [of the Security Council] opposed giving the prosecutor this power' (Hall, 1998a: 132). Other opponents included India, Indonesia, Iran, Japan and Mexico (Benedetti and Washburn, 1999: 19).

In the same session, the Security Council's blocking power was discussed. While many states (according to one civil society participant, 'the overwhelming majority') favoured deleting this provision, the permanent members of the Security Council, and in particular the

United States and France, insisted on leaving it in (Benedetti, 1997). A compromise proposal first made informally a year earlier by the Singaporean delegation leader Lionel Yee attracted much attention. This proposal, widely believed to have emanated from Yee's own brilliant legal mind rather than from the Singaporean bureaucracy (interviews Pace, Dicker), turned the ILC provision on its head. Instead of the Security Council having to *approve* a prosecution, and hence being subject to permanent member vetoes, it would have to take a majority decision to *block* any prosecution. Any exercise of the veto could only be used to prevent a decision to block, and would therefore be in favour of going ahead with prosecutions, not for stopping them. According to observers, three permanent members of the Security Council – China, the Russian Federation and the United Kingdom – and a significant number of states that would have preferred to delete the paragraph altogether expressed interest in the proposal. Some states suggested that the Security Council should be able to prevent a prosecution for twelve-month renewable periods (Hall, 1998a: 131; Benedetti and Washburn, 1999: 20). The 'Singaporean proposal' was included in the draft Statute, in brackets, as an alternative to the original provision, and revisited in Rome.

The fifth PrepCom session in December 1997 did not officially deal with trigger mechanisms. Nonetheless, it was precisely this session that saw several breakthroughs that made the independent prosecutor into a much more realistic option. First of all, the prosecutor of the Yugoslavia tribunal, Louise Arbour, visited the PrepCom and made a 'dramatic and forceful address . . . which appears to have made a deep impression on the thinking of government delegates on crucial issues, including the role of the Security Council and of the prosecutor' (Hall, 1998b: 339). Second, the Like-Minded Group developed its cornerstone positions, and an independent prosecutor able to initiate proceedings was one of them. Finally, the United Kingdom, now under a Labour government, showed signs of changing its position, stating that 'although it had always been mindful of the burden on the prosecutor of having to act on his or her own initiative, it was now listening closely to what other delegations had to say about this proposal' (Hall, 1998a: 132). On the Security Council's blocking power, it went even further, saying it would oppose this provision and support the Singaporean proposal instead. This was the first crack in the previously united opposition of the permanent members of the Security Council to the independent prosecutor.

In their advocacy papers published before the Rome Conference, major human rights organisations such as Amnesty International, the

Fédération Internationale des Droits de l'Homme, Human Rights Watch and the Lawyers Committee for Human Rights all continued to insist on deletion of the provision allowing the Security Council to block prosecutions, rather than accepting the Singapore compromise (Broomhall, 1998: 14).

Giving the prosecutor authority to proceed on his or her own initiative, subject to review by a pre-trial chamber of judges, became a formal Argentine–German proposal in April 1998, and remained in the draft that went to the Rome conference. However, the entire article was still in brackets, which meant that some states objected, and the whole text might yet be struck. It was generally agreed that the powers of the prosecutor was one of the very sensitive matters which could not possibly be agreed upon before the Rome conference (Wilmshurst, 1999; Hall 1998a: 130; Benedetti and Washburn, 1999: 18).

The Rome conference

The opening of the Rome conference saw another permanent member of the Security Council making positive noises about the independent prosecutor as well as the Singapore proposal. The French Foreign Minister, Hubert Vedrine, who attended the opening days of the conference in person, gave explicit support to the idea of an independent prosecutor whose intended prosecutions would be subject to review by a pre-trial chamber, calling it an 'innovative solution' ('Dutch Disbelief', 1998). His support for the Singapore proposal was more equivocal, and subject to further conditions ('Dutch Disbelief', 1998; Haq, 1998c). The United Kingdom, on the other hand, was 'accused of backtracking on Council referral' and showing only 'luke-warm support for an independent prosecutor' ('"Rebellious" Rome Conference', 1998). The United States, China and Russia remained opposed to an independent prosecutor and against the Singapore proposal, although the silence of the United States on the latter issue in an opening speech raised the expectations of some observers (Haq, 1998a).

A week into the conference, the United States published a position paper outlining its opposition to an independent prosecutor. Instead of painting a picture of a politicised or maverick prosecutor as it had earlier done, it now portrayed an overwhelmed one, unable to deal with the overload of cases coming to his or her attention (United States, 1998). However, the next day Richard Goldstone, former prosecutor for the International Criminal Tribunal for the former Yugoslavia (ICTY), visited the negotiations. His very presence suggested that prosecutors allowed to make their own choices can work effectively, and in a speech he threw his weight behind the independent prosecutor, subject to review by a pre-trial chamber (Jackson, 1998b; Guest, 1998). Another day later, the US-based Lawyers Committee for Human Rights hit back with a twenty-eight-page document rebutting the arguments of the United States against an independent prosecutor as well as drawing attention to inaccuracies in the US paper (LCHR, 1998c).

From the beginning of the conference, the CICC kept a precise tally of how many and which countries took positions on the most important issues before them. Thus, it was reported that on Monday, 22 June, fifteen out of twenty-eight countries spoke in favour of an independent prosecutor, and on Tuesday a further thirty-nine did so, with twenty-four countries speaking against. Brazil, Mexico and Venezuela were among the states shifting in favour, with Kenya going the opposite way. Algeria, India, Nigeria, Pakistan, Syria, Turkey and Uruguay remained against (Haq, 1998c; 'Support Growing', 1998). This counting exercise made it visible for the first time just how much state support there was for an independent prosecutor. The coordinator of the Coalition, Bill Pace, commented that while a year earlier the independent prosecutor had seemed like a utopian option, now a majority of states supported it (Haq, 1998c).

In the next two weeks of negotiations, while minor issues were being resolved, there was very little movement on key issues such as the prosecutor. The Canadian chair therefore called a closed meeting of thirty-odd 'key' states at the embassy on a Sunday to discuss a confidential proposal. According to one source, this proposal contained only one option on trigger mechanisms, listing states, the Security Council and the prosecutor him- or herself as the triggers ('The Compromise Package', 1998). However, 'on the same evening, the text was substantially modified by Kirsch in order to reflect some U.S. positions' (Benedetti and Washburn, 1999: 29), and the Bureau Discussion Paper published on the basis of these negotiations two days later contained both this option and that of having just states and the Security Council (Bureau Discussion Paper, 1998: draft art. 12). On the blocking power of the Security Council, however, the paper included only the Singapore proposal and an option allowing for no blocking power at all. The former suggested the blockage would be valid for a twelve-month period, renewable by another Council resolution (ibid.: draft art. 10).

The next few days were devoted to gathering comments about the proposal, and the CICC again recorded which states were in favour of each option. Sixty-one of the eighty states speaking were in favour of the prosecutor's own initiative (CICC, 1998b). Eighty-three per cent of all states supported two variants of the Singapore proposal ('CICC Team Reports', 1998). The United States remained consistently against the independent prosecutor, but indicated willingness to accept the Singapore compromise. Delegation leader David Scheffer tried to raise the stakes by stating, on the one hand, that his delegation would recommend US ratification of a treaty that was favourable to the US position on crucial issues, but, on the other hand, that the United States would actively oppose a treaty that was not (Haq, 1998g; 'The US Shows Its Hand', 1998).

The next Bureau Proposal maintained the first option, of a prosecutor subject to a pre-trial chamber, but instead of an option 2 deleting this article, option 2 only suggested unspecified 'additional safeguards' to make the independent prosecutor more palatable (Bureau Proposal, 1998: draft art. 12). On blocking powers, it added a provision whereby the Security Council itself would decide how long it would block a prosecution, rather than there being a fixed limit (ibid.: draft art. 10). The CICC recorded that sixty-three states now supported the proposal to have an independent prosecutor, with or without further safeguards, while just thirteen states remained opposed (CICC, 1998c). A significant majority of fifty-three states supported Singapore-style Security Council blocking power for twelve months, with just five states prepared to let the Council itself specify the time limit, and fourteen holding out for no blocking power at all (ibid.).

After the explicit acceptance by the United States, and wide approval from other states, the Singapore proposal regarding the Security Council's blocking power for a renewable twelve-month period appears to have been a done deal. Its inclusion, unchanged, in the final package, was no surprise. Human Rights Watch representative Richard Dicker commented, 'I saw that coming a mile away' (interview Dicker). Having officially insisted on removal of the Security Council's blocking power altogether before the conference, the major human rights organisations now apparently contented themselves with the Singapore compromise. Their last joint appeal, a few days before the end of the conference, no longer mentioned it, while a Human Rights Watch appeal even gave it explicit support ('An Appeal from Four Major Human Rights Organizations', 1998; 'Human Rights Watch Appeal', 1998).

Further negotiations were conducted on the principle of an independent prosecutor. However, 'an informal round of negotiations led by Brazil failed to specify further safeguards, as most states simply reiterated their support for, or opposition to, the prosecutor's power to proceed on his own initiative' (Fernández de Gurmendi, 1999: 186). At this point, the negotiations became increasingly informal and untransparent. Canadian negotiators Kirsch and Holmes write that the inclusion in the second Bureau Proposal of the 'additional safeguards' option, instead of the option of having no independent prosecutor at all, 'was rightly seen as an indication that the battle against the independent prosecutor was lost, and the issue began to pale in comparison to other jurisdictional issues' (Kirsch and Holmes, 1999: 27).

However, this was by no means clear to human rights activists at the time. The CICC coordinator later commented that 'I don't think anyone knew what was going on that last week except John Holmes, the Canadian ambassador, Kirsch, and some key leaders of the Like-Minded Group, until very late Thursday night' (interview Pace). According to an academic observer, 'Kirsch kept the options open until the very last day, and even slightly before, it was impossible to say what was going to happen' (interview Schabas). Human Rights Watch representative Richard Dicker remarked that 'in the last few days it really went subterranean . . . in the closing hours, the last day or two, there were rumours that the *proprio motu* was going to be deleted from the package deal; we expected that that might happen' (interview Dicker).

In response to these rumours, the 'major international human rights groups then formed mixed teams – Human Rights Watch, Amnesty, the ICJ, the Lawyers Committee – to approach specific delegations with this message, so it didn't come from one particular group by itself, it was a very important theme for all of us. We put a great deal of emphasis on it, with credible representatives, so it would not be sacrificed' (interview Dicker).

The final package presented to the conference by the chair, Philippe Kirsch, did indeed include three trigger mechanisms for the Court: referral by the Security Council, referral by a state, and initiation by the prosecutor him- or herself, subject to authorisation by a pre-trial chamber of judges. NGO representatives did not fully comprehend at the time that this was indeed the final package; they thought that there might be further concessions, or on the other hand that elements of the draft might yet be strengthened (interviews Pace, Dicker). Hence, their reactions to the Statute as a whole were initially very critical. The press release by the Lawyers Committee for Human Rights did not even mention the prosecutor, focusing only on the faults in the proposal (LCHR, 1998d; AI, 1998b; HRW, 1998b). They were not alone in believing amendments were still possible. The US delegation leader,

David Scheffer, later wrote that 'on 17 July, I spent the entire day consulting with a large number of governments and explaining that the opportunity still existed to seek reasonable modifications to the bureau's final text' (1999: 21).

However, the Like-Minded Group supported the final package, and spent the day lobbying to have it adopted without further changes, and an unchanged package was put before the conference the same Friday evening. Interestingly, the United States did not seek to challenge the principle of having an independent prosecutor, but instead proposed an amendment concerning jurisdiction (see Chapter 4). India proposed a number of changes, including deleting the provision on the Security Council's blocking power. These challenges were quickly headed off by a vote to take no action on them. The same package was put to a final secret vote (at the request of the United States) later that evening, and adopted at 10 p.m.

In NGO press releases after the vote, the independence of the prosecutor was the first point to be mentioned as a 'major victory'. Some criticism was levelled at the adoption of the Singapore compromise, rather than the absence of any blocking power for the Security Council at all, but the most trenchant condemnation was reserved for the final package's solutions on jurisdictional issues, as discussed in the next chapter (AI, 1998c; HRW, 1998c; LCHR, 1998e).

Conclusion

This major victory, and the compromise regarding the Security Council, were not, of course, won by global civil society alone. They would have been impossible without the imaginative proposals on the pre-trial chamber and the inversion of the Security Council vetoes, put forward, by Argentina and Singapore respectively. The great strength of both proposals was their eminent reasonability: they addressed the legitimate and express concerns of particular states, without pandering to their not so legitimate and implicit concerns.

The Singaporean proposal addressed the concern expressed especially by the permanent members, that the Security Council should not be constrained in exercising its core task of maintaining or restoring international peace and security, for instance by a prosecutor upsetting sensitive peace negotiations with indictments. Meanwhile, it did not, of course, address the unspoken desire of each permanent member of the Security Council to reserve the power to block prosecutions it considered detrimental to its interests. This, however, was not an argument they could make publicly with an appeal to the international community's common interest. The Argentinian proposal addressed fears of a 'maverick prosecutor' by limiting his or her powers, but it put these powers into the hands of an independent panel of judges, instead of states or the Security Council. This safeguard was difficult to argue against without suggesting that the entire panel of judges could be 'maverick'. Thus, it again stripped state arguments of rational appeal and legitimacy, laying bare self-interested resistance to an active prosecutor and an effective court.

The global civil society contribution to the adoption of the Singapore compromise can only be considered minor. Possibly, the consistent – but not very high-profile – opposition of NGOs to any Security Council blocking power, shared by a few non-aligned states, helped to put the Singapore proposal in middle position, rather than being the only alternative to the original veto powers in the ILC draft.

The contribution to the independent prosecutor was much more substantial, as acknowledged by diplomats involved in the negotiations. The Dutch delegation leader called it 'the most important point on which the NGOs booked success' (interview Van Boven), and Kirsch and Holmes include 'the proprio motu role of the prosecutor' among 'just some of the features that might not have appeared without concerted NGO insistence' (1999: 36).

This contribution began many years before the Rome conference, with the detailed position papers of major human rights organisations on the matter. On the one hand, these showed by precedent that there were reasons to believe the ICC would have very little work without either an independent prosecutor or a victim complaint mechanism. On the other hand, they rebutted the idea that this was a radical innovation in international law by pointing at individual complaints procedures in the human rights treaties and to the relative independence of the prosecutors of the *ad hoc* tribunals. They continued to debate with reluctant states, notably the United States, on the substance of their arguments all the way through. The Lawyers Committee's response, within two days, to a US position paper at the Rome conference is a prime example.

Bringing in the possibility of a victim-triggered system, in analogy to the individual complaint mechanisms under human rights treaties, served to move the initially most radical proposal of an independent prosecutor closer to the centre ground. According to a member of the NGO Coalition for an International Criminal Court,

> it was clearly understood by the majority of the Coalition that it was unlikely for States to agree to individuals having the capacity

> to initiate proceedings. However, such a 'radical' suggestion made the prospect of an independent Prosecutor appear more acceptable and less threatening than that of individual citizens 'triggering' the Court. An independent Prosecutor was thus seen as a less extreme option.
>
> (Durham, 2000b, unpublished)

The credibility of this tactic was strengthened by the fact that a few states also referred to this option, so threatening to others, early on in the negotiations.

A second global civil society contribution to the independent prosecutor was made by the past and present prosecutors, and staff, of the Yugoslavia and Rwanda tribunals. According to an academic observer, William Schabas, the 'case for an independent prosecutor was immensely strengthened by the extremely positive model of responsible officials presented by Richard Goldstone and Louise Arbour, the *ad hoc* tribunals prosecutors who held office while the Statue was being drafted' (Schabas, 2001: 97). But theirs was not just a passive contribution, demonstrating by example that an independent prosecutor was viable. Both took part in conferences during the PrepCom years, and intervened in the negotiations at crucial times with speeches arguing that, on the basis of their experience, there was a greater likelihood of the ICC's prosecutor being impotent than omnipotent. These speeches appear to have made an impression on hesitant state representatives.

The growing number of NGOs that became members of the CICC and threw their weight behind the independent prosecutor during the years leading up to the Rome conference raised the profile of the issue to one of the key topics of negotiation. According to the Argentinian delegate Silvia Fernández de Gurmendi, an early and active member of the Like-Minded Group of states, who chaired the negotiations on this issue and had frequent contact with NGOs, 'Non-governmental organizations led a strong campaign in favor of conferring such power as an essential feature of an independent, credible Court. The issue became a central point in the discussions' (1999: 177).

It is impossible to say for certain whether the principle of an independent prosecutor was still in danger in the final days of the conference and whether, therefore, the joint démarche by major human rights organisations made a difference in this respect. It is certain, however, that a final package without an independent prosecutor would have been universally condemned by the NGO and individual members of the CICC. It had become their number one issue, their 'collective bottom line'. The chair, Kirsch, was undoubtedly well aware of this, and chose not to alienate them.

Beyond its own collective stance on the prosecutor, the CICC sought constantly to strengthen and make more visible the state support for having an independent prosecutor. Many state delegates would concede that an independent prosecutor was desirable, but they needed to be convinced that it was also politically possible. This was done by demonstrating the existing support for the position and, by demonstrating this, continuing to build on it.

All through 1997, the Coalition pressed the LMG to assert itself and show its hand by formulating its guiding principles. In December 1997, it finally did so, and the prosecutor's own initiative was one of those principles (Pace, 1999: 206; Benedetti and Washburn, 1999: 21, 23).

During the Rome conference, it continued this tactic by continually analysing the statements made by delegates, and transposing them into virtual votes on different positions. Despite the fact that it had a stake in a certain outcome, this 'barometer' function of the CICC was apparently credible to state delegates. This showed, at various points in the conference, that a large and growing majority, finally of 83 per cent (of those states whose delegates took the floor and spoke), was in favour of the independent prosecutor. This focus on the numbers counteracted the customary tendency of negotiators of concentrating on 'powerful states', in this case particularly France, the United Kingdom and the United States.

According to Richard Dicker of Human Rights Watch,

> [T]hat bit of work of accurately recording, and putting together immediately, where each state stood on the major issues, was the single greatest contribution of the NGOs. Each state might have done it, except they didn't really have the capacity, we spent late nights . . . getting it out into the newsletter, getting it to the delegates, and they faxed it to their capitals, that was crucial, stiffening the resolve by accentuating the number of states that wanted an effective independent court.
>
> (interview Dicker)

International law cannot be made without the consent of states. The independent prosecutor could not have become a feature of the International Criminal Court without the approval of a large majority of states. However, global civil society played a crucial role, first, in persuading states that *proprio motu* powers of the prosecutor were desirable, and second, in persuading them that it was achievable because they wanted it. It is safe to say that without the global civil society campaign, the independent prosecutor would not have made it into the Statute.

4 The defeat

No universal jurisdiction

Types of jurisdiction

Apart from the 'trigger mechanism' described in Chapter 3, there was another hurdle the Court would have to clear before being able to try a case: jurisdiction. Jurisdiction, according to a legal dictionary, is 'the power or authority of a court to take cognisance of matters put before it and to decide such matters' (Walker, 1980: 678). It has many different aspects, which I briefly discuss before turning to the two most controversial aspects for the rest of the chapter. The related issue of complementarity or admissibility is discussed in Chapter 3.

Temporal jurisdiction (the time from which crimes committed would fall under the jurisdiction of the Court) was a relatively minor issue: in line with the principle of legal certainty, it was generally agreed that the Court would only try crimes committed after it had come into existence. Some NGOs argued that since the crimes in question were already crimes under international law before the Court existed, this principle was not at stake, and in fact the Nuremberg, Tokyo, Yugoslavia and Rwanda tribunals had all tried crimes retroactively. Nonetheless, there was no serious attempt to give the Court retroactive jurisdiction. According to Schabas, 'the idea was unmarketable and was never seriously entertained during the drafting' (2001: 57).

Personal jurisdiction was also relatively uncontentious: although some states would have preferred a lower age limit, and others a higher one, in accordance with their own legal systems, it was agreed that only persons who were at least 18 at the time of commission of the crime could be tried before the Court. As mentioned in Chapter 2, there was an attempt by France and the Solomon Islands to include 'legal persons' – that is, non-state entities, which might include corporations or NGOs – as suspects, but this received little support (Arsanjani, 1999: 61–62).

Subject-matter jurisdiction attracted much more discussion. As discussed in Chapter 1, the original proposal by Trinidad and Tobago concerned drug-related crime. However, a brief list of widely agreed crimes for the jurisdiction of the Court began to crystallise early on, and it did not include drug crimes. The crimes that were included were genocide, crimes against humanity and war crimes. Other crimes, particularly drug-related crimes and terrorism, were repeatedly proposed for inclusion, but never received substantial support (Von Hebel and Robinson, 1999: 80–81, 86–87; Schabas, 2001: 28). The crime of aggression was a major bone of contention between states, partly because there is no agreed definition of aggression in international law, and partly because no agreement could be reached on whether there should be a role for the Security Council in determining whether aggression had occurred (Von Hebel and Robinson, 1999: 81–85). The positions in civil society were divided, and on the whole muted, on the issue of aggression. As the CICC coordinator explained, 'Many NGOs would like to see aggression included, but are wary of doing so because of the power it would give the Security Council' (Dickens, 1998). The final compromise solution in the Statute is that aggression is included as a crime, but cannot be adjudicated by the Court until a definition is agreed by the states parties.

The other bone of contention in relation to subject-matter jurisdiction was whether war crimes committed in internal conflicts (as opposed to international ones, which was uncontentious) would come under the jurisdiction of the Court. This was a substantial advocacy topic for civil society, and Kirsch and Holmes include it on their list of 'features of the statute that might not have appeared without concerted NGO insistence' (1999: 36).

Civil society groups and individuals, particularly the Red Cross, human rights groups and individual lawyers, also made a substantial contribution to the precise definitions of the crimes, both in the Statute and in the more detailed Elements of Crimes negotiated in June 2000 (see Meron, 1999; Schabas, 2001: 29–53).

However, in order not to overload a complicated topic still further, this chapter will deal with only two jurisdictional issues which remained extremely contentious until the very end of the negotiations: the manner in which states would bestow jurisdiction on the Court ('acceptance of jurisdiction'), and which state's jurisdictional consent is required for the Court to try a case (referred to as 'exercise of jurisdiction' or 'state consent').

Acceptance of jurisdiction

Acceptance of jurisdiction comes into play when a state ratifies the Statute: does this also mean it automatically accepts the Court's jurisdiction over all the crimes that are in the Statute, or would states have the choice of accepting jurisdiction for some crimes but not others, or for some time period only, or on a completely case-by-case basis? The former is, for instance, the system of the European Convention on Human Rights, ratification of which by a state means that the European Court of Human Rights automatically has full jurisdiction over any alleged breaches of the Convention by that state. The latter is the system of the International Court of Justice, which adjudicates disputes between states, for which there is in fact no separate ratification procedure.

The 1994 draft by the International Law Commission left states very free on how much jurisdiction they would accept: after ratification of the Statute, each state could make a declaration, declaring for which crimes it would accept jurisdiction, and for what periods of time. It could also choose to accept jurisdiction only in relation to particular incidents, committed during a specific time period. If it accepted jurisdiction for an indefinite time period, it could withdraw such acceptance with six months' notice. These provisions were usually referred to in the negotiations as an 'opt-in' system, or sometimes, particularly by those who did not like the system, as jurisdiction 'a la carte' (Hall, 1998a: 131). The only exception was genocide, for which, as discussed below, a complaint could be brought by a state, and accepted by the Court, without acceptance of jurisdiction being necessary.

The first comprehensive Amnesty International report on the ICC, published a few months later, deviated from the ILC draft and proposed 'inherent' jurisdiction over 'a common core of grave crimes', as opposed to the opt-in system: by ratifying the Statute, states would automatically accept the Court's jurisdiction over these crimes, which in its conception should include genocide, crimes against humanity and war crimes (AI, 1994: 17–18). This was called 'inherent' because jurisdiction was to be inherent in the act of ratification itself, instead of needing a separate procedure. However, as will be discussed below, this term led to some confusion, and later on in the negotiations the term 'automatic jurisdiction' was preferred to describe the same concept. The ICJ also supported the idea of inherent jurisdiction for genocide, crimes against humanity and war crimes, pointing at legal precedents. Interestingly, it cited a US position taken in relation to the Yugoslavia tribunal to support this position (ICJ, 1995: 27–28).

In the first *ad hoc* committee in March 1995, the Like-Minded Group countries Argentina, Austria, Denmark, Germany, Greece and Sweden suggested that the 'inherent jurisdiction' idea should be extended beyond genocide. Japan and India on the other hand resisted the idea even for genocide. Australia and the United Kingdom supported a general 'opt-in' regime on the basis that it would ensure broad ratification of the Statute. Finland instead suggested 'opt-out' – that is, that there should be inherent jurisdiction unless a state made a declaration to the contrary (ICJ, 1995: 27, n. 114–116, 123–125; UN, 1995d: paras 90–102). In the August 1995 session, Switzerland formally proposed a regime of inherent or automatic jurisdiction through ratification for all the Statute's crimes. In the April 1996 PrepCom, the same proposal was tabled by the German delegation (Kaul, 1998: 368). A majority of states now supported this proposal, but a significant minority continued to oppose it (Wilmshurst, 1999: 131).

During 1996 and 1997, more NGOs (though not nearly as many as spoke out on the prosecutor) gave their views on the issue of jurisdiction. Human Rights Watch and the Lawyers Committee for Human Rights followed Amnesty and the ICJ in pleading for inherent jurisdiction for the three core crimes, arguing that crimes against humanity and war crimes are almost impossible to separate from genocide, that inherent jurisdiction would simplify the jurisdiction regime and that it would make for a more effective Court. This trend culminated in the adoption by the CICC of inherent jurisdiction as one of its Basic Principles (CICC, 1998a).

The cornerstone positions of the LMG of states, promulgated in December 1997, also included 'inherent' jurisdiction for the three core crimes. In the last PrepCom session in March 1998, the United Kingdom, now a member of the Like-Minded Group, made a comprehensive proposal covering a number of aspects of trigger mechanisms and jurisdiction. It also supported inherent jurisdiction rather than opt-in.

In the first week of the Rome conference, Germany, the United Kingdom and South Korea all made proposals which differed on the issue of state consent, as is discussed later in the chapter, but which all suggested that acceptance of jurisdiction should be inherent or automatic. This option was increasingly supported by a large number of states, with the exception of France, which was emerging as a vocal proponent of opt-in (Haq, 1998e).

There was little movement on major jurisdiction issues until the Sunday meeting called by the chair after three weeks (see Chapter 1), and the Bureau paper published two days later. This gave a number of options, including both the opt-in system and automatic jurisdiction, and hybrid options with automatic jurisdiction for some crimes but not others. In the open meetings of the next few days, the CICC monitored and published the support for each option. Many African and other Like-Minded states (73 per cent of all the states that took a position) expressed a preference for automatic jurisdiction, but France, China and the Arab states continued to insist on opt-in (Kirk, 1998b). The United States and Russia accepted automatic jurisdiction for genocide, but wanted opt-in for war crimes and crimes against humanity.

The next Bureau proposal, three days later, gave only two options on acceptance of jurisdiction: either the CICC/Like-Minded option of automatic jurisdiction for all three core crimes, or the original ILC option of automatic jurisdiction for genocide with opt-in for crimes against humanity and war crimes. According to the CICC's 'virtual vote', three-quarters of states favoured automatic jurisdiction, with the remaining one-quarter preferring option 2, combining automatic jurisdiction for genocide with opt-in for war crimes and crimes against humanity. France continued to insist on an opt-in regime, but now only for war crimes ('French Position on War Crimes', 1998). While the major human rights organisations focused on state consent (see the next section), the Red Cross statement published at this point was particularly vocal in its opposition to an opt-in regime ('Opting In on War Crimes', 1998).

At this point, Philippe Kirsch asked the Japanese ambassador, Hisashi Owada, to undertake informal consultations. His consultations seem to have focused on the idea of a separate protocol arranging an 'opt-out' regime. Since the negotiations were confidential, it is not clear whether this referred only to acceptance of jurisdiction, or whether it also had implications for state consent. What is clear is that most of the Like-Minded Group considered this option fundamentally unacceptable (Kirk, 1998c; Wilmshurst, 1999: 137). Normally, separate protocols are intended for states that wish to take on additional obligations beyond a treaty – they are therefore referred to as additional or optional protocols. This peculiar proposal was sneeringly called a 'subtractional protocol' instead (Bergsmo, 1998: 347).

Subsequently, in secret negotiations France proposed a renewable ten-year opt-out of jurisdiction for war crimes and crimes against humanity. This deal was not put to the entire conference, but only to a smaller group of EU and other Like-Minded states. Germany headed a counter-proposal which included whittling down the French proposal to a one-off three-year opt-out for war crimes only (Kaul, 1998: 371–373). The final 'take-it-or-leave-it' Bureau package presented the night before the end of the conference chose automatic jurisdiction through ratification, but one exception was made to bring France on board: a special clause allowing a one-off seven-year opt-out for war crimes (Art. 124, ICC).

NGO reactions to this compromise were very severe. The Red Cross called it 'a hollow stone in the construction of the Court', the Lawyers Committee on Human Rights said it would 'severely hamper its effectiveness for years, if not decades' and Amnesty International said it gave soldiers a 'license to kill with complete impunity' (ICRC, 1998b; LCHR, 1998e; AI, 1998b).

With hindsight, this seems like an overreaction. As the same NGOs have often pointed out, the core crimes are often interrelated, and where there are war crimes severe enough to meet the thresholds of the ICC, there may be crimes against humanity too. Moreover, the opt-out can only be taken advantage of at the moment of ratification, and it is non-renewable, so any opt-outs will eventually run out, and the provision will become a dead letter. The main achievement, of an inherent jurisdiction regime, will remain. Finally, out of the ninety-seven ratifications to date, only France itself and Colombia have actually made use of the opt-out (this may be partly due to the NGO campaign against it). US-based groups have even begun to use the provision in their advocacy campaigns to convince the US public that it would have nothing to fear from the Court if it were to ratify the Statute (UNA USA website; WICC website).

State consent

Early negotiations

Unlike acceptance of jurisdiction, state consent becomes relevant only once there is a suspect who might be put on trial. Suppose, for instance, a Saudi Arabian is suspected of crimes against humanity committed on Ugandan soil, but the victims of which include Australian nationals, and the suspect is arrested in Morocco. Then which country would have to give consent (*ad hoc* or by ratification) for the ICC to be allowed to try the case? This could be Saudi Arabia (the state of nationality or 'suspect state'), or it could be Uganda (the territorial state). These two are the primary principles operating in many domestic criminal systems. More unusual options could include Australia (victim state) or Morocco (custodial state). Exercise of jurisdiction could be widened by allowing consent from just one of various possibilities to suffice. Or it could be narrowed by insisting that the consent of a combination of 'states with an interest' would be necessary. Consent can be given by a state in two ways: either by ratification, dependent on the rules of acceptance of ratification (see p. 63), or on an *ad hoc* basis: a state that has not ratified then gives consent only for the specific case at issue. Finally, there was the possibility of arguing that (because of the seriousness of the crimes) no form of state consent was necessary at all. This is the universal jurisdiction principle. If this were adopted, the discussion on acceptance of jurisdiction would also become superfluous.

The International Law Commission's draft statute of 1994 provided two regimes for state consent: if the case concerned an accusation of genocide, the Court would have jurisdiction if a complaint had been brought by any state that had ratified the Genocide Convention, and no further consent would be needed. Such a complaint could therefore bypass acceptance of jurisdiction, as discussed above. This was because the Genocide Convention, concluded in 1948, explicitly gives jurisdiction to an international criminal court, which, it was thought at the time, would be established soon. If the case did not involve genocide, consent from the state where the alleged crime had taken place (territorial state) *and* the state that had custody of the suspect (custodial state) was required. In the example above, therefore, there would need to be ratification or *ad hoc* consent from Uganda and Morocco, while the position of Saudi Arabia and Australia would be irrelevant. However, referral by the Security Council would override the need for such consent.

The Amnesty International report of 1994, one of the first NGO documents to feed into the ICC negotiations, peculiarly enough did not deal with the issue of state consent, but instead devoted a section to state obligations to 'extradite or try' suspects of particular crimes. This may have been because the complementarity regime was not yet negotiated, and at the time it seemed possible that a national prosecution would completely block the ICC from prosecuting – although this was not envisaged in the ILC draft (AI, 1994: 18–21). The language used by the International Commission of Jurists (ICJ), the next organisation to publish a lengthy report on the ICC, is also confusing on the issue of state consent. It appears to limit itself to advocating 'inherent' jurisdiction for core crimes. However, it is not entirely clear what is meant by 'inherent' jurisdiction in this context. It could simply mean, as discussed above, that acceptance of jurisdiction by a state automatically came with its ratification of the Statute. Or it could mean that jurisdiction is inherent in the nature of the crime. This would mean arguing that certain crimes, including genocide, crimes against humanity and war crimes, are so heinous that the Court has jurisdiction to try cases concerning these crimes regardless of state consent (ICJ, 1995: 27–28, 34). Such proposals built on the doctrine of 'universal jurisdiction', which teaches that such crimes, because they 'shock the conscience of mankind', can be tried by any court anywhere in the world.

This confusion is not only apparent in this ICJ document. It was widespread and bedevilled much of the negotiations on jurisdiction. The records of the 1995 Ad Hoc Committee meetings noted that, while it was clear that most delegations were referring to 'jurisdiction inherent in ratification', rather than 'jurisdiction inherent in the nature of the crimes', some states pointed at the danger of conflation between inherent and universal jurisdiction, as in the ICJ document (UN, 1995d: para. 92).

Apart from this confusion, there was also a wide range of views among states. Some argued that the state of nationality of the accused (Saudi Arabia in the example above) should be added to the list of states required to consent. Thailand and India even required that 'all states who had an interest' would have to consent. Other states including Italy and Denmark defended the ILC proposal against such restrictions. Switzerland suggested that only the custodial state (Morocco in the example) would have to consent, and Austria suggested that no consent was needed at all where horrific crimes such as genocide, crimes against humanity and war crimes were concerned (ICJ, 1995: 137–138; n. 145–150; UN, 1995d: paras 103–111).

PrepComs

In 1996, Human Rights Watch published its own first comprehensive ICC report. It explicitly proposed that no consent from any state should be required – that is, that the Court should have universal jurisdiction. A later document by the Women's Caucus for Gender Justice also proposed a jurisdiction both inherent and universal. The Lawyers Committee, like Amnesty, remained silent on this issue at this point (HRW, 1996: 5–6; LCHR, 1996: 16–17; WC, 1997a: 4–6). One of the strongest documents in support of universal jurisdiction at this time was a paper by the International Committee of the Red Cross, enumerating the precedents for recognising universal jurisdiction for each of the three core crimes in national legislation, international treaties, national and international case law, customary law and scholarly writings (ICRC, 1997b).

State consent was again addressed by states in August 1997. In this session, Samoa was the first state to suggest, as a number of NGOs had by then advocated, that the crimes to be covered in the Statute were already subject to universal jurisdiction under customary international law. If any state's domestic courts had authority to try cases of genocide, crimes against humanity and war crimes, then the ICC, which was precisely to be set up for this purpose, should have such authority too. No state consent should be needed.

France proposed the opposite extreme, namely that consent would have to be given by the state where the crime was committed *and* the state of nationality of the suspect *and* the state of nationality of the victim *and* the state that was holding the suspect (Hall, 1998a: 131). In the example cited above, consent would be needed from Uganda and Saudi Arabia and Australia and Morocco.

As seen above, the principles of the Like-Minded Group of states included 'inherent' jurisdiction for the three core crimes, but, like many NGOs, they remained silent on state consent. So again, the term 'inherent' was – accidentally or deliberately – ambiguous: some took it to be equivalent to universal jurisdiction, while for others it just meant automatic acceptance of jurisdiction, and said nothing about state consent.

In 1998, there was further civil society support for inherent or automatic jurisdiction, coupled with further confusion over state consent. The American Bar Association, for instance, adopted a resolution stating that 'The ICC's exercise of jurisdiction over the core crimes should be automatic, meaning that no additional declaration of consent (other than ratification of the ICC treaty) should be required.' It remained unclear, however, whose consent by ratification was required for a case to be tried (ABA, 1998: 3). The European Parliament, too, adopted a resolution which 'stresses that inherent jurisdiction should be extended to cover all the "core crimes", genocide, crimes against humanity, and war crimes', but remained silent on state consent (EP, 1998). During the Rome conference, it would adopt another unanimous resolution, this time pleading explicitly for universal jurisdiction ('European Parliament', 1998).

In the last PrepCom session in March 1998, the United Kingdom, now a member of the LMG, made a comprehensive proposal covering a number of aspects of trigger mechanisms and jurisdiction. On state consent, it proposed, like the original ILC draft, that jurisdiction should be based on consent from both the territorial state and the custodial state. Germany, another member of the Like-Minded Group, submitted a proposal espousing universal jurisdiction (Wilmshurst, 1999: 132). It became clear that no resolution would be reached on jurisdiction during the PrepCom negotiations. As a result, a variety of opt-in, opt-out and inherent jurisdiction proposals, and various permutations of state consent, were included in the draft text in brackets, which became very convoluted as a result (ibid.: 131).

Rome conference

Only in May 1998 did influential organisations like Amnesty International and the Lawyers Committee for Human Rights spell out that the Court should have both automatic jurisdiction *and* universal jurisdiction. The latter organisation devoted a whole paper to the issue (AI, 1998a; LCHR, 1998b). This expanded focus of the NGOs was also reflected in the 'Basic Principles' the CICC adopted just before the Rome conference, which contained automatic or inherent jurisdiction as its second principle and universal jurisdiction as its third (CICC, 1998a). The president of the International Committee of the Red Cross, who was given the opportunity to address the opening session of the conference, made universal jurisdiction one of the main points of his speech ('State Consent Could Weaken the Geneva Convention', 1998). In Rome, the Coalition formed a special team (named the state consent team) to monitor and report on the negotiations on jurisdiction.

South Korea became the third Like-Minded state to develop a proposal on state consent. It was floated as a possible compromise between the British and the German options. It was based on the very restrictive French proposal made a year earlier, but subverted its meaning by changing all the 'ands' to 'ors': consent from the state of nationality of the suspect *or* the state where the alleged crime had taken place *or* the state of nationality of the victim *or* the state holding the suspect was enough. In the example used throughout this chapter, this would mean that consent from Saudia Arabia or Uganda or Australia or Morocco would suffice to allow the hypothetical case to get to the Court. This was more restrictive than the German universal jurisdiction proposal in principle, but would have given the Court an almost equally strong position in practice. The inclusion of the custodial state was especially important: it made the position of any other state irrelevant, as long as the state actually holding a suspect were willing to give him or her up (Kaul, 1998: 368–369). The United States immediately made it clear that neither the German nor the Korean proposal was acceptable. The same position was taken, bien é tonné, by Cuba ('US, Cuba Thumb Down Compromise', 1998).

Most states tended to reserve their positions on the crucial jurisdiction issues, however, and no progress was made until the closed weekend meeting at the Canadian embassy after the third week of the conference (Wilmshurst, 1999: 134). After that meeting, the US ambassador, David Scheffer, met conference chair Philippe Kirsch, insisting that more had to be done to accommodate American concerns, and reportedly insisted in particular that state consent must be based solely on the nationality of the suspect ('US Launches Long-Awaited Preemptive Strike', 1998).

The subsequent Bureau Paper listed no fewer than four options on state consent: the (Korean) or/or/or/or option; the British option of consent from the territorial and custodial state; an alternative British option of consent from the territorial state only; and a US-inspired option insisting on consent from the state of nationality of the suspect only. In terms of the example, the first option would require consent from Uganda or Saudi Arabia or Australia or Morocco for the case to come to court; the second option would require consent from Uganda and Morocco; the third option from Uganda only; and the fourth option from Saudi Arabia. The German option of universal jurisdiction, or no consent, was not included (Bureau Discussion Paper, 1998: draft art. 7). As noted by both conference newspapers at the time, 'By removing the option that gives the Court the greatest jurisdiction . . . the discussion paper makes South Korea's compromise proposal one of two extremes, and therefore favours the British compromise' (Haq, 1998f: 8–7; see also 'US Launches Long-Awaited Preemptive Strike', 1998).

As recorded by the CICC, 23 states expressed explicit regret in subsequent discussions about the exclusion of universal jurisdiction. The South Korean proposal had the support of 79 per cent of the states that took the floor. The United States made it clear that it considered its own option, of consent from the state of nationality of the suspect, as the only acceptable one (Kirk, 1998b; Haq, 1998g).

The next Bureau proposal, published a few days later, offered yet more complicated permutations, making the consent regime again dependent on the crime, as it had been in the original ILC draft. For genocide, it proposed only one option: the Korean proposal of the territorial or the victim or the suspect or the custodial state. For war crimes and crimes against humanity, there remained three options: the Korean one-of-four proposal, the British proposal of the territorial and the custodial state, and the US proposal of the suspect state only (Bureau Proposal, 1998: draft art. 7). The German proposal for universal jurisdiction was not reinserted.

Immediately afterwards, on the last Monday of the conference, Amnesty International, the Women's Caucus, Human Rights Watch and the Lawyers Committee for Human Rights launched both a joint and four separate appeals to the conference on the main issues still at stake. Amnesty and the Women's Caucus continued to insist on universal jurisdiction, while Human Rights Watch and the Lawyers Committee gave qualified support to the Korean option. The joint statement stated that there 'should be no preconditions . . . more restrictive than' the Korean option ('An Appeal from Four Major Human Rights Organizations', 1998). The Red Cross made a separate statement focusing particularly on automatic jurisdiction, but, beyond that, also insisting on the principle of universal jurisdiction ('Opting In on War Crimes', 1998).

According to the CICC's 'virtual vote' tally, support for the South Korean one-of-four proposal for all three crimes had now grown to 85 per cent (CICC, 1998c). Those states which would have preferred universal jurisdiction now agreed to support this option instead (Wilmshurst, 1999: 136). Only eleven states spoke in favour of the other two options.

At this time, the conference reverted to informal negotiations, including attempts to broker a deal by the Japanese ambassador and closed negotiations between the five permanent members of the Security Council. The CICC coordinator Bill Pace 'knew that the P-5 [the permanent members of the Security Council] were having meetings, but the details of what they were suggesting were secret' (interview Pace). It was not just civil society representatives who were kept in the dark, however. The Spanish delegation leader too complained publicly about a 'lack of transparency regarding the package that will be presented to delegations', and expressed concern about the fate of the jurisdiction regime in particular ('Where Are Decisions Being Made?', 1998). A German delegate's – clearly furious – account of behind-the-scenes negotiations in the last two days of the conference nonetheless gives a reasonably clear picture of what happened (Kaul, 1998; see also Scheffer, 1999: 19–20 and Wilmshurst, 1999: 137–138, for more opaque accounts).

On 15 July, the permanent members of the Security Council (P-5) met to join forces to push through their own preferences. This package included territorial jurisdiction only (the United Kingdom), a possibility to withhold jurisdiction when the suspect state recognised the crime as an 'official act' (the United States) and a renewable ten-year opt-out of jurisdiction for war crimes and crimes against humanity (France) (Kaul, 1998: 371–373). The package was informally presented to the Bureau and the other EU states the next day. The latter did not like it, and most supported an informal German counter-proposal reinstating the South Korean option, ignoring the US 'act of state' proposal and, as already stated, reducing the scope of the French opt-out.

After this confrontation remained without result, the chair, Kirsch, decided in his 'take-it-or-leave-it draft' to combine the original British and US options, or, to put it differently, to chop the Korean proposal in half: consent from either the suspect state *or* the territorial state (Saudi Arabia or Uganda in the example) was the provision included in the final package, while custodial and victim state options were left out. The 'official act' clause of the United States was not included.

The United States rejected the final package on a number of counts, but its ambassador's

> most impassioned argument concerned the issue of jurisdiction, which has been the key concern all along for the Americans. Scheffer said that the ICC will be able to exercise jurisdiction over non states parties. This, he said, would be a fundamental violation of the principle that states cannot be obligated to a treaty they have not joined.
>
> ('A Court Is Born', 1998)

As described in previous chapters, the United States and India introduced amendments on the last evening of the conference, which were overwhelmingly defeated by a no-action motion; the US amendment tried again to exclude territorial jurisdiction for official missions (Wilmshurst, 1999: 139).

Many NGOs were equally passionate in their condemnation of the final jurisdiction regime. Amnesty International issued the strongest statement, opening with

> Saddam Hussein, Pol Pot, Karadzic, Pinochet, Amin, Mobutu. These are just some of the men responsible for the worst crimes in the world whose prior consent would have been required in order for them to be tried under the statute for a permanent international criminal court.
>
> (AI, 1998c)

Human Rights Watch said the provision would 'dramatically reduce the number of cases that the court can act upon', and, alluding to the exclusion of consent from the custodial state, called it a 'passport for travelling tyrants' (HRW, 1998b, c). Other organisations, too, reserved their worst criticism of the Statute for the jurisdiction regime (LCHR, 1998d; interviews Dicker, Donat-Cattin, Pace).

Conclusion

Negotiations concerning the jurisdiction regime for the ICC were extremely complicated. They concerned the two separate but linked issues of acceptance of jurisdiction and preconditions for the exercise of jurisdiction, or state consent. Myriad options were bandied about, sometimes concerning one, sometimes both issues. It appears that neither all state representatives nor all groups and individuals in civil society fully understood all the options at all times. On the contrary, it is likely that only a very few individuals had a complete command of the subject.

The first issue, that of acceptance of jurisdiction, presented relatively few problems. Automatic jurisdiction for genocide, war crimes and crimes against humanity had been an important priority for the legal and human rights organisations involved in the Court campaign from the beginning. Their position papers gave states a number of substantive arguments for this position, including the – by no means incontrovertible – argument, which came to be widely repeated and accepted, that this was an accurate reflection of existing international law. Automatic jurisdiction became one of the guiding principles adopted by the Like-Minded Group at the urging of the NGOs, and by the beginning of the Rome conference most states that called themselves like-minded, and some that did not, supported it. What bedevilled the negotiations was the expression 'inherent jurisdiction', which meant automatic jurisdiction for some, but nothing less than universal jurisdiction for others.

As seen above, NGOs did not formulate a united and comprehensive position on the exercise of jurisdiction until just before the Rome conference, after Germany had already formulated its proposal for universal jurisdiction in the PrepCom. During the conference, the monitoring and reporting activities of the CICC's 'state consent team' were hindered by the fact that, in the discussions, some states pronounced a preference on the issue of acceptance, some on state consent, and some on both issues. Moreover, there was a plethora of possibilities, comprising all the different 'and' and 'or' combinations between four possible states with an interest in a case. In the early stages, states often expressed 'sympathy' for more than one option.

All this made both internal lobbying and public advocacy very difficult. The jurisdiction issue was as vital to the effectiveness of the Court as the role of the prosecutor. But in sharp contrast to the issue of the prosecutor, where the basic choice and its consequences could be explained to any interested outsider in a few sentences, the negotiations on jurisdiction were hard to follow, let alone explain and translate into a simple, compelling demand.

Later on in the conference, as the number of options became more limited, NGOs were faced with the uneasy choice between supporting the German proposal for universal jurisdiction and the South Korean proposal. While the German proposal was the principled progressive position, the more pragmatic South Korean proposal, while less of a bold step forward in international law, also opened the possibility of a court with extensive powers of jurisdiction. In general terms, it is an unresolved question whether it is better in negotiations to have a 'maximalist' position, or to plump for a reasonable compromise. In this particular case, a stronger lobby from the NGOs might have prevented the premature deletion of the German proposal from the Bureau package, which moved the South Korean option from a compromise to a 'most radical' position. It is clear that no strategic choice was made by the Coalition or by the four major organisations that made a final joint appeal in favour of one option or the other. Hence, this appeal wavered between the two options.

Nevertheless, by 13 July, when the CICC published its last 'vote count', the Korean proposal looked like a winner. Eighty-five per cent of states expressed a preference for it. Even if the Coalition's advocacy was not as strong as it might have been, its information function was sending a very clear message. The fact that this proposal did not make it into the Statute was due to a reversion, accepted by the chair, to old-fashioned diplomatic methods which were out of character with the rest of the negotiations in two ways.

First, there was the reversion to secrecy. NGOs, the media and in fact most state delegates had no access to these last-minute negotiations (Kaul, 1998; interviews Dicker, Pace). While some were aware that the permanent members of the Security Council were cooking up a proposal, the details were not known. When the P-5 proposal was presented to a select group of Like-Minded states the day before the end of the conference, they expressed fierce opposition, but did not break the confidentiality, even though it might have been in their interest to do so. Thus, the avenue of allowing global civil society to mobilise public indignation against a P-5 dictate, both within the conference and beyond, was not opened. Admittedly, the time for such an offensive would have been very short, but immediate mobilisation in urgent situations is precisely one of the strengths of global civil society networks.

Second, the preferences of a large majority of states likely to ratify the Statute were largely disregarded in favour of a deal between a few 'most powerful states'. With respect to the one-off war crimes opt-out for France, this deal, while inelegant, does not detract from the effectiveness of the Court in a serious and lasting way. The solution on state consent, however, intended to be a compromise between the wishes of the US government on the one hand and the wishes of most other states and civil society groups and individuals on the other, has turned out to be the worst of all worlds. It has led to a jurisdiction regime that pleases no one. Its exclusion of more extensive bases of jurisdiction, such as consent by a custodial or a victim state, will hamper the Court's effectiveness. At the same time, its inclusion of consent by the territorial state, instead of the state of nationality of the suspect only, has caused the United States to launch a fierce multi-pronged offensive against the Court.

5 The controversy

Gender and forced pregnancy

The recurrent clash

As has been discussed by various scholars from a legal perspective, the Statute for an International Criminal Court is 'the first international treaty to recognize a range of acts of sexual and gender violence as among the most serious crimes under international law' (Steains, 1999: 357; see also Bedont and Hall Martinez, 1999; Boon, 2001; Oosterveld, 1999). This chapter focuses on how the gender provisions came into the Statute, discussing the ICC negotiations as a critical episode in the recurrent clash within global civil society between the women's movement and the 'pro-family' movement.

The terms 'women's movement' and 'pro-family movement', used in this chapter, are of course oversimplifications. Both movements are pluralistic, consisting of many smaller alliances which are sometimes at odds with each other. These terms, rather than others, are employed here because they are among the most frequently used self-identifying terms of both groups, but without endorsing the possible connotations they might appear to have: that all women are represented by the former, or that those who are not part of the latter are somehow 'anti-family'. The term 'pro-family' was preferred over 'pro-life' because the concerns of these groups at the ICC extended beyond abortion, including opposition to the use of the term 'gender'. The term 'women's groups' was preferred over 'feminist groups' because most organisations prefer this over the narrower and polarising term 'feminist', even though they would probably subscribe to some form of feminist value system if pushed on the matter.

While confrontations between women and patriarchal powerholders are as old as the hills, national policy debates about sexuality and birth control in particular emerged in the West with the second generation of women's movements in the 1960s and 1970s. The issue of abortion became the prime matter of controversy, especially in the United States. Various authors have discussed the subsequent transnational debates over feminist priorities, and the eventual convergence of many women's groups around the issue of violence against women, the controversies they faced and the strengths of what is now a vibrant global women's movement (Bunch *et al.*, 2001; Sen, 2003; Friedman, 1995; Joachim, 1999; Keck and Sikkink, 1998).

However, little attention has been paid to the fact that pro-family groups, both Protestant and Catholic but always supported by a globally oriented Catholic Church, have also come to form a transnational movement, which confronts the women's movement at every UN forum that has any relevance to sexual and reproductive issues (some attention is paid to this movement by Kulczycki (1999: 25–28) and Keck and Sikkink (1998: 189–191)). There is a clear need for further research into the beliefs, tactics and leadership of this movement generally. Such research will be helpful in understanding that global civil society is not the exclusive domain of 'progressive' human rights, environmental, social justice and women's rights activists; it is a space co-inhabited by conservatives, anti-abortionists and religious fundamentalists.

The surfacing of two social movements with contradictory aims at the same venue highlights the significance of recurring questions about global civil society participation in international fora: Who is legitimate? Who is representative? Who has a right to be there? Women's groups have been confronted with diverse voices from within the movement, but they still tend to be collectively considered at UN fora as the sole representatives of women's concerns. Some pro-family groups explicitly question this notion. REAL (Realistic Active for Life) Women of Canada, for instance, argues:

> No one organization or ideology can represent the views of all women any more than any one organization can represent the views of all men. Until the formation of REAL Women of Canada, there was no voice to represent the views of those many thousands of women who take a different point of view from that of the established feminist groups.
>
> (REAL Women website)

The remainder of this chapter looks into the claims to legitimacy and representativeness of both types of groups, as well as the manner and success of their lobbying activities, in the negotiations on the International Criminal Court.

The two movements at the ICC negotiations

Women's groups

Two sets of transnational advocacy experiences informed the strong interest women's groups came to have in international criminal law. On the one hand, this interest built on the UN conferences, often described as crucial to the emergence of a global women's movement. After the earlier conferences of the UN Decade for Women (Mexico City 1975; Copenhagen 1980; Nairobi 1985) had played a major role in building women's networks, it was particularly at the World Conference on Human Rights in Vienna in 1993 and the Fourth World Conference on Women in Beijing in 1995 that progress was made in actually inserting gender concerns into the final declarations of the conferences (Bunch *et al.*, 2001: 219–221; Keck and Sikkink, 1998: 186–188). These were not treaty-making conferences, however, and the challenge for women's rights groups was to take the progressive texts of these 'aspirational' declarations into the 'mainstream big-boy venue of hard-core international law' of the ICC negotiations (interview Hall Martinez; cf. also Steains, 1999: 360).

On the other hand, experiences with the Yugoslavia tribunal were a particular inspiration to women's groups' advocacy for an international criminal court. While it had been pointed out before that women are always particularly vulnerable to abuse in conflicts (see, for instance, Erb (1998: 401–402) for a harrowing catalogue of war-related violence against women in the twentieth century), the use of rape as a component of ethnic cleansing in the former Yugoslavia brought the lack of legal protection to international attention (Steains, 1999: 359). Although the statute of the Yugoslavia tribunal did not contain any gender-specific mandate, its functionaries recognised that an ostensibly gender-neutral justice system would in fact fail to address gender-specific abuses, and took on board some of the concerns of women's groups. An officer for gender issues was appointed within the prosecutor's office, and it was decided to allow rape victims to give testimony anonymously, and to prosecute rape as a war crime, an issue to which the first prosecutor, Richard Goldstone, was particularly committed (Sharratt and Kaschak, 1999: 12–13, 31, 54). It was in their relations with the tribunal in The Hague that Yugoslav women and their international supporters had their first experience of enscribing women's concerns into international criminal law, an experience they built on at the ICC negotiations in New York and Rome. Later, the Akayesu case before the Rwanda tribunal provided further illustrations to the case for gender justice: the suspect was convicted of genocide in the form of systematic rape and sexual violence after probing but sensitive questioning of witnesses by the only female judge, Navi Pillay (Bedont and Hall Martinez, 1999).

As described in Chapter 2, the main civil society interest in the ICC negotiations came from human rights organisations, while lawyers, global governance organisations, peace groups and faith-based organisations were also represented. While some women's groups, such as Equality Now, had been involved since the first state negotiations on the ICC in 1995, most were relative latecomers to the process (EN, 1995). The Women's Caucus for Gender Justice was formed at the initiative of a small group of women's rights activists present at the February 1997 PrepCom, who realised that without a much stronger effort, gender concerns were not going to be adequately represented in the negotiations. It quickly grew to be a coalition within a coalition, with hundreds of member organisations by the time of the Rome conference (Bedont and Hall Martinez, 1999; Durham, 2000a: 829).

While the Women's Caucus was born out of the idea that gender concerns were not adequately represented by members of the existing Coalition, the Coalition did support the organisation and lobbying efforts of the Women's Caucus, made it a member of its Steering Committee, and eventually adopted as one of its Basic Principles that the ICC 'should ensure that all aspects of its work take gender concerns into account' (CICC, 1998a).

The Women's Caucus could accurately claim to be representative of a global audience, as shown by a geographic breakdown of the women's organisations accredited to the Rome Conference (Figure 5.1). This figure gives only a very partial picture of the make-up of the Women's Caucus, for two reasons. First, it is only a snapshot of organisations present at Rome, not showing organisations which were active before and after Rome, or were active only at the domestic level. Second, the Women's Caucus was a network of individuals and organisations, and this figure shows only the latter. But in the Women's Caucus, as in the Coalition more generally, individuals did play a substantial role. One of the founder members of the Caucus, for instance, the feminist lawyer Rhonda Copelon, based at the City University of New York, was not affiliated to any NGO. Nevertheless, Figure 5.1 shows that women's groups from every region were represented, with the exception of North Africa and the Middle East, and that groups from the South formed a majority. The lack of representation from the Middle East followed a general trend, described in Chapter 2. In many of the countries in this region, there is generally limited political space for civil

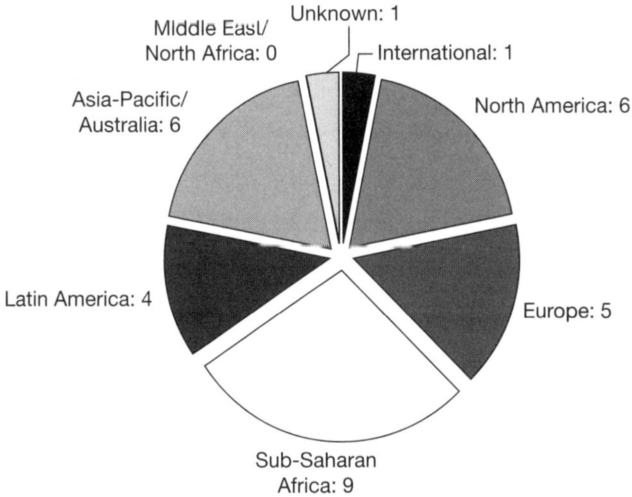

Figure 5.1 Women's groups at Rome: regional distribution.

society groups to operate freely, and the situation for progressive women's organisations is even bleaker.

The Women's Caucus was highly visible in Rome: it had between twelve and fifteen people at the conference at all times (Facio, 1998: 3–4). The delegation, moreover, included both women from conflict areas and experts on the 'hard-core legal stuff' (interview Hall Martinez). While the former could speak with moral authority about violations of women's rights, the latter could invoke emerging precedents in national and international law. The Women's Caucus was also able, because of its large numbers and energy, but also its natural advantage in often – but by no means inevitably! – finding allies in female state delegates, to get many states on its side. One member of the Caucus mentions Australia, Bosnia, Canada, Costa Rica, Mexico, the Netherlands, European countries generally, South Africa for ten Southern African countries, and Sweden as being among the countries the Caucus had very good relations with (interview Hall Martinez). This list is particularly formidable because it includes the two countries chairing the negotiations (first the Netherlands and later Canada), two other countries that chaired working groups on different parts of the Statute (South Africa and Sweden), and the country chairing the special negotiations on gender issues, Australia. One person from the Women's Caucus (the 'snake'; see p. 84) became a member of the Canadian state delegation; another went on the delegation of Costa Rica (Facio, 1998:

14). All this suggests that there was a strong overlap in values and aspirations between the Women's Caucus and the so-called Like-Minded Group of states which drove the negotiations.

Pro-family groups

While abortion is the primary focus of the pro-family movement, some of the groups it comprises also campaign against euthanasia, contraception and cloning, promote what they call a Christian approach to politics, encourage women to be homemakers, advocate for marriage and against cohabitation and homosexual and transsexual lifestyles, and favour the prohibition of prostitution and pornography (see websites REAL Women, C-FAM, CLC, HLI). In the last two areas, their aims are by no means diametrically opposed to those of all parts of the women's movement (see Sen, 2003: 138–140, 145 on divisions within the women's movement over the sex industry).

At least one pro-family group, the Catholic Family and Human Rights Institute, has a permanent office at the United Nations in New York, and keeps a close eye on all UN processes that touch on its concerns. Its aims include 'act[ing] as a liaison and network referral service on behalf of similar organizations worldwide' (C-FAM website). In November 1997, this group published an appeal by the Vatican for stronger involvement of pro-family NGOs in UN conferences. A month later, it warned that 'the strong presence of many feminist NGOs in the preparation for the upcoming ICC conference' should be of concern to pro-family activists (C-FAM, 1997a, b).

The pro-family groups came to the scene even later than the Women's Caucus. They came not just with an anti-abortion agenda, but also with concerns about 'forced social change by feminist, homosexual and other radical groups' (Campaign Life Coalition quoted in 'ICC: Promise of Justice or Threat of Tyranny?', 1998). While they came to the negotiations in order to oppose what they saw as dangerous proposals by the Women's Caucus, they did not so much strive for a Statute that would reflect their concerns, as oppose the agreement of a Statute and establishment of a Court generally, as 'many pro-lifers also see the court as a crucial step in the abandonment of national sovereignty, and the establishment of a tyrannical world government' ('ICC: Promise of Justice or Threat of Tyranny?', 1998).

It is difficult to establish exactly how many pro-family groups attended the Rome conference, because of the peculiar accreditation procedure for this conference, described in Chapter 2, which saw the CICC coordinator, Bill Pace, vetting groups for accreditation.

However, it was also made possible for groups who did not wish to go through this procedure to apply directly to the UN official in charge of organising the conference, Roy Lee: 'a few came in directly through Roy Lee; sixteen or so were added to the list in that way' (interview Pace).

At least two pro-family groups, REAL Women of Canada and the International Right to Life Federation, were accredited through the CICC (UN 1998). Others may have been accredited directly through the United Nations' legal office. Finally, particularly because of the special privileges accorded to pro-family groups through their close links with the Vatican (see pp. 84–5), it is also possible that there were groups present and lobbying that were not properly accredited. Either way, it is clear that at least two more groups were in Rome: the Campaign Life Coalition from Canada, and the Catholic Family and Human Rights Institute (Evans, 1998; C-FAM, 1998a). According to one participant, Human Life International was also there, which seems likely as it is the largest international pro-family organisation (interview Hall Martinez; HLI website).

Although this may not be an entirely exhaustive list of the pro-family groups represented, two things stand out immediately in the comparison with the women's groups: there were far fewer of them, and they appeared to come from only two countries: Canada and the United States. Although the views of the pro-family contingent may be shared by many worldwide, the groups actually at the ICC negotiations were very far from being globally representative in the same way that the Women's Caucus was. As the Canadian pro-family publication LifeSite Daily News acknowledges,

> During the conference, the Women's Caucus outnumbered the pro-life/family contingent and were well-prepared and effective in their lobbying of the normally pro-family African and South American delegates. . . . The small band of pro-family lobbyists . . . was prevented from achieving even more because of a crucial absence of any Spanish-speaking members and having only two French-speaking members [presumably Canadians].
>
> ('Lifesite Report', 1998)

The tolerance of the NGO Coalition for an International Criminal Court for a wide range of views among its members went beyond accreditation: it allowed the pro-family groups to participate in its meetings and make use of its facilities unless it became clear that they were hostile to the idea of a just, effective and independent court, in which case it would 'try to have such groups leave through the back door' (interview Pace). While tolerated by the Coalition, the pro-family groups were not exactly welcomed. Most NGOs and many state delegates greeted them with irritation and hostility. The Australian delegate who chaired negotiations on gender issues, for instance, called their lobbying an 'unfortunate departure from the generally constructive role played by NGOs throughout the Conference' (Steains, 1999: 368).

However, they also had some very strong state allies, particularly in the Vatican and to a lesser extent other Catholic and Arab countries (Bedont and Hall Martinez, 1999; C-FAM, 1998c). Their links with the Vatican gave them a privileged position: they were given their own office in the building of the Food and Agriculture Organization in Rome, where the negotiations took place, while all other NGOs had to share one room, and very few state delegations had offices (interviews Pace, Hall Martinez). According to one source, moreover, it was rumoured that the Pope personally placed phone calls to leaders of Latin American countries on the issue of forced pregnancy (interview Hall Martinez).

Relations between the two movements

Relations between representatives of the women's groups and the pro-family groups were an exception to the general spirit of camaraderie among civil society delegates to the Rome conference. They can be described as hostile, even vitriolic. Members of the Women's Caucus have described the involvement of the opposition as an 'intense and sustained attack by an alliance of religious fundamentalists and conservative organisations' (Oosterveld, 1999: 39), 'intent on undermining the Court's ability to appropriately address sexual and gender crimes', by making 'misleading linkages' (Bedont and Hall Martinez, 1999: 67).

The pro-family groups usually referred to the opposition simply as 'feminists' or 'radical feminists' (probably a swearword in their circles), but occasionally they became more venomous: one article, for instance, claimed that a Canadian Women's Caucus member was being referred to as 'the snake' by state delegates (REAL Women, 1998b), while another referred to the women's groups as the 'anti-life, anti-family movement' ('ICC: Promise of Justice or Threat of Tyranny?', 1998).

Both sides accused the other of having privileged access to certain state delegates. The women's movement complained about the close links of the pro-family groups with the Vatican, and in particular that, as already mentioned, the pro-family groups were given their own office. The pro-family groups complained that two members of the Women's Caucus had been made members of the official delegations of Canada and Costa Rica, and more particularly that the Women's Caucus had been allowed to address a closed 'informal' meeting of thirty states at the Canadian embassy, a grievance discussed in a number of pro-family publications (Evans, 1998; REAL Women, 1998b; 'Rome Conference Ends without Consensus', 1998).

A member of the Women's Caucus also made more damaging accusations that 'a bunch of them has UN accreditation, but their tactics are dirty. They will make hand-outs with no name of the group on it, which is against the regulations' and 'they would for instance dump a pile of . . . documents into the garbage'. She acknowledged, however, that this did not apply to all pro-family groups: 'other groups also disagreed with us, other Catholics, but they were tolerant, they played by the rules' (interview Hall Martinez).

The issues

The original draft for the ICC, drawn up by the International Law Commission in 1994, paid no explicit attention to the gender dimensions of any of the areas of law it covered (ILC, 1997). This reflected the existing state of humanitarian law and international criminal law, as codified in the The Hague and Geneva conventions and the statutes of the *ad hoc* tribunals for Yugoslavia and Rwanda. The practices and jurisprudence of these tribunals between 1995 and 1998 were beginning to change this situation, however, and provided inspiration for the demands of the women's rights groups united in the Women's Caucus for Gender Justice (Steains, 1999: 359).

Gender concerns related to many parts of the Statute. This chapter focuses on two of them: the use and definition of gender, and inclusion of a sub-paragraph on gender-specific crimes, including forced pregnancy, in the definition of war crimes and crimes against humanity. Other concerns of the women's groups, including references to the gender balance and gender-specific expertise of the judges and other staff of the Court, a reference to gender in a general non-discrimination clause, a gender dimension to the definition of slavery, the inclusion of persecution on the basis of gender as a component of crimes against humanity, and protection for and gender-sensitive treatment of victims and witnesses, are not dealt with here. All these concerns, however, came to be reflected in the Statute in a way that either completely or partially satisfied the Women's Caucus (Bedont and Hall Martinez,

1999; Oosterveld, 1999). The set of concerns of the pro-family groups was much narrower, as is discussed later in the chapter.

Use and definition of gender

The Women's Caucus wanted to integrate a gender perspective into the entire Statute, and specifically to use the term 'gender', for two reasons. First,

> [I]t is precisely because the vast majority of laws, legal instruments and institutions have been created without a gender perspective that the everyday violations of women's human rights are invisible to the law and the most atrocious violations have been rendered trivial.

Second,

> [S]ince the vast majority of those who commit the crimes or are responsible for them are men, one of the probable causes of these crimes may well be the social construction of the masculine gender and therefore one of the solutions may well lie in creating mechanisms that will help construct less violent men.
>
> (Facio, 1997: 10)

The women's groups involved in the ICC negotiations came primarily out of the movement to combat violence against women, and the issue of gender crimes was therefore their primary focus. However, they also had institutional concerns, such as having a 'gender balance' in the panel of judges, as well as gender expertise among the judges and in the prosecutorial office.

Pro-family groups objected to the use of the term 'gender' anywhere in the Statute. One group expressed fears that it might 'provide protection for "other genders" including homosexuals, lesbians, bisexuals, transgendered, etc' (REAL Women of Canada, 1998b). Another group went even further, stating that use of the term gender 'could be interpreted as criminalizing any national laws or policies that favor heterosexual marriage over homosexual couplings, on the grounds that homosexuality is a recognized "gender"' (C-FAM, 1998b).

The pro-family groups did not begin to challenge the term 'gender' until the early weeks of the Rome conference, when many, especially less controversial, clauses of the Statute had already been decided upon (Oosterveld, 1999: 39). Hence, the term has been retained in article 7 (persecution on the basis of gender as a crime against humanity), article 21 (no gender discrimination in the application of the Statute), article 42 (gender expertise in the prosecutor's office) and articles 54 and 68 (treatment and protection of victims and witnesses). In other instances, however, the pro-family groups succeeded in excising the g-word. The Statute now speaks of 'a fair representation of female and male judges' and 'the need to include judges with legal expertise on specific issues, including, but not limited to, violence against women and children' (Rome Statute, 1998: articles 36.8 (a) iii and 36.8 (b)). While this really makes no difference to the substance of the first of these clauses, women's groups would argue that 'expertise on gender violence' is broader than 'expertise on violence against women', as it also encompasses violence targeted specifically against men, whether it be forced recruitment, execution or sexual violence. Even 'violence against women and children' was unacceptable to some delegates, but at this point the delegate from Burundi made an emotional appeal, describing the experiences of his own country, and insisting that special attention to women and children must not be abandoned (Steains, 1999: 382).

After protracted negotiations, in which some delegates (and their civil society supporters) insisted that the term 'gender' be rejected altogether, while others (and the Women's Caucus) insisted that the term was in general use throughout UN documents, and generally understood, the following definition of gender was agreed: 'the term gender refers to the two sexes, male and female, within the context of society. The term gender does not indicate any meaning different from the above.' The Australian coordinator of these negotiations later wrote:

> While the Statute's definition of 'gender' appears, on its face, to be rather unusual (with the tautological second part of the definition), it represents the culmination of hard-fought negotiations that managed to produce language acceptable to delegations on both sides of the debate. At the end of the day, it was the only definition of 'gender' to which the Arab states and others were willing to agree. At the same time, the reference to 'within the context of society' satisfied those delegations that wanted the definition to encapsulate the broader sociological aspects of the term, along the lines of earlier definitions.
>
> (Steains, 1999: 374–375)

Forced pregnancy and other gender crimes

Deciding which crimes should be subject to the Court's jurisdiction, and how they should be defined, was one of the core issues in the ICC negotiations. Early proposals relating to the definition of crimes made scant reference to rape as an 'outrage on personal dignity', and none to other gender-related crimes. This changed with a joint proposal in February 1997 by New Zealand and Switzerland to include rape directly as a war crime. This proposal was taken over almost verbatim from a paper by the International Committee of the Red Cross (ICRC, 1997a), reflecting developments in the Yugoslavia tribunal in particular. The Women's Caucus was just beginning to be formed at that time, and did not play much of a role. The United States, however, favoured a more restrictive definition of war crimes in general, and the whole text remained bracketed. At the same time, 'rape, other sexual abuse and enforced prostitution' were included, unbracketed, as a crime against humanity (Hall, 1998a: 127–128).

In a paper for the December 1997 PrepCom, the Women's Caucus first proposed a separate sub-paragraph on sexual and gender crimes in the definition of war crimes, which was to include 'rape, sexual slavery, forced prostitution, forced pregnancy, forced sterilization and other sexual or gender violence or abuse'. It recommended this extra paragraph partly on the basis of the prosecutorial practices of the Yugoslavia and Rwanda tribunals, because 'sexual and gender violence are severe and particular and their particularities should not be lost by mainstreaming. Where not explicit, they are too often ignored, even today' (WC, 1997b). The sub-paragraph adopted by this PrepCom, which was substantially more comprehensive than the earlier proposals, mirrors almost exactly the wording proposed by the Women's Caucus in their preparatory paper, and it can safely be assumed to have been proposed at their instigation. It was included without brackets in the draft text on war crimes for the Rome conference – that is, it reflected widespread consensus among states, despite an objection from the Vatican to 'enforced pregnancy' (PrepCom, 1997). In the next PrepCom in the spring of 1998, the Vatican sought to replace the term with the more restrictive 'forcible impregnation', the implication of which was that it was the impregnation alone that was criminalised, not any attempt to coerce the woman to carry the baby to full term (Steains, 1999: 364–366).

Pro-family groups joined the Vatican in voicing objections to the inclusion of forced pregnancy as a war crime, calling it a 'code word for criminalizing any denial of access to abortion' (C-FAM, 1998d). To support this view, they cited a US domestic lawsuit against the state of Utah, in which the American Civil Liberties Union had defined the term as 'forcing women to continue pregnancy against their will for the purpose of serving the state's declared interest in preserving unborn human life' – that is, to describe an anti-abortion law or policy (REAL Women, 1998a). Although supporting the Vatican's 'interim maneuver', pro-family groups were hoping that 'the language will be dropped altogether, and UN veterans cite growing sentiment even among liberal delegations to do just that' (C-FAM, 1998a).

This became the most contentious gender issue at Rome, with opponents, including the Vatican and some Catholic and Arab states, arguing that making enforced pregnancy a crime implied a state obligation to permit abortion. Proponents of the clause, including many Western states, but also conflict states like Bosnia and Rwanda, and Muslim states such as Azerbaijan and Turkey, argued that it was meant to codify a terrible crime, such as witnessed in Bosnia, and had nothing to do with viewpoints on abortion (Steains, 1999: 366). Bosnia issued a paper documenting the practice and calling for retention of enforced pregnancy as a separate crime in the Statute, and lobbied other Muslim countries on the issue (Oosterveld, 1999: 39; 'National Abortion Laws', 1998).

After three weeks in Rome, an informal working group was formed, chaired by an Australian delegate, to bring the two positions on gender-related issues closer together and to try to define forced pregnancy in a mutually satisfactory way. The definition that came out of these negotiations in the final week of the conference was

> the unlawful confinement of a woman forcibly made pregnant, with the intent of affecting the ethnic composition of any population or carrying out other grave violations of international law. This definition shall not in any way be interpreted as affecting national laws relating to pregnancy.

The second sentence was clearly inserted to protect the anti-abortion laws of the objecting countries (Steains, 1999: 366–368). The subparagraph was then included both in the war crimes section and in the crimes against humanity.

Conclusion

The original draft Statute by the ILC made no use of the word 'gender', and contained no articles that could be characterised as gender sensitive. Without the advocacy of the Women's Caucus, the term 'gender' and most of the gender provisions would probably not have made it into the Statute, although again they were immensely helped by the experiences of the Yugoslavia tribunal. The insertion of the clause on gender crimes into the treaty can certainly be ascribed to the influence of the Women's Caucus. However, its preservation over strong opposition, against forced pregnancy in particular, owed more to a few crucial state representatives than to the Women's Caucus, although the Caucus's statement in Rome that 'this will not affect national abortion laws' ('National Abortion Laws', 1998) may have been helpful. The strong advocacy of Bosnia, which had the moral high ground on this issue, and the patient but tough negotiating by Australia kept the comprehensive clause on gender crimes in the Statute.

The pro-family groups' main tactics had been to equate use of the term 'gender' with endorsement of homosexuality (an argument strengthened by the fact that 'gender' is difficult to translate into other languages, including Arabic), and use of 'enforced pregnancy' with support for the right to abortion. This probably had some impact in the last preparatory negotiations and early in Rome, but it was countered by the tactic developed by the Australian delegate of negotiating an agreed definition to both terms to allay fears of such interpretations. Once such definitions had been agreed, their role was pretty much played out, and although the Women's Caucus might have preferred more progressive definitions, it cannot be said that the pro-family groups had a noticeable influence on the contents of the Statute.

The case study on gender justice in the ICC therefore challenges a pervading sense in the women's movement generally that those who work on gender concerns are necessarily always disadvantaged and marginalised. The UN High Commissioner for Human Rights, Mary Robinson, echoed this idea when she congratulated the Caucus for 'overcoming intense opposition from many representatives' in ensuring that gender violence was included in the Statute (Robinson, 2000). This sense of women's activists being the underdog, undoubtedly justified in many local, national and international settings, should not be assumed to be applicable to every situation, however.

The Women's Caucus did not, in fact, meet with intense opposition from many representatives; it met with intense opposition from very few representatives. The Women's Caucus may initially have had to overcome indifference and lack of understanding from many delegates, but it did not meet with widespread hostility. Moreover, the hostility that it did meet did not come from the permanent members of the Security Council or the Like-Minded Group, whose position on the

ICC was considered crucial in the negotiations, but from the Vatican, a few Arab states and, in the case of forced pregnancy, some 'Catholic' states, with Ireland playing a particularly prominent role (see Bedont and Hall Martinez, 1999: 75, n. 44, for a full list of states with objections to forced pregnancy). As discussed earlier, it had a powerful list of allies among state delegates, some of which, including Canada, the Netherlands and South Africa, were the main drivers of the negotiations. It also had the backing of the CICC, which worked closely with the Like-Minded Group of states.

Despite their close links with the Vatican, it was, in fact, the pro-family groups that were marginalised at this particular forum. The coordinator of the CICC speaks of 'the very large majority of advanced women's organisations and a minority of organisations absolutely devoted to preventing any international policy that would in any way endorse abortion' (interview Pace). As demonstrated in the quotation of the Australian delegate on p. 84, they were disliked not just by the NGOs, but generally by the 'Like-Minded' delegates in favour of a strong international criminal court, who realised that while the pro-family groups were at the negotiations primarily to influence debate on gender issues, they did not favour the establishment of an international criminal court generally.

I do not wish to suggest that these groups did not deserve to be marginalised, or that they should have been made more welcome by states or civil society actors. Since not only their narrow aims, but indeed their whole worldview, were diametrically opposed to that of most state and civil society delegates at the conference, that was not to be expected. However, it should be recognised that global civil society is not a harmonious entity with a single set of shared values. It is populated by actors with strongly held values, 'organising to influence their world' (see Chapter 1), but these strongly held values are not all the same. They may diverge or even clash. Plurality and even discord are part and parcel of global civil society.

What is remarkable about this case study is that compromises were in fact found, in multilateral negotiation, that satisfied both these diametrically opposed groups to a reasonable extent. As a result of the compromises reached, the Women's Caucus and the pro-family groups could both claim victory. The definition of gender is described in one publication as a compromise produced by 'hard work from pro-lifers', although 'the phrase "within the context of society" worries some pro-lifers, who fear it will be used to get around the qualification, and to promote redefinitions of marriage and family' (Evans, 1998). A leading member of the Women's Caucus, on the other hand, writes that the definition 'is unfortunate, [but] having the term in a legal or "hard" international document as opposed to a policy or "soft" document . . . is a gain for real justice' (Facio, 1998: 6).

In the case of forced pregnancy, members of the Women's Caucus celebrated the fact that the 'Rome Statute is the first international treaty specifically listing the crime of forced pregnancy' (Bedont and Hall Martinez, 1999); while a pro-family group pointed out that 'virtually all the sting has been removed . . . courtesy of strictly limited definitions' (C-FAM, 1998d). While both positions had gained something in the compromise, it is clear that the results were more disappointing for the pro-family groups. While publications by members of the Women's Caucus bear titles such as 'The Making of a Gender-Sensitive Court' (Oosterveld, 1999) and 'Ending Impunity for Gender Crimes' (Bedont and Hall Martinez, 1999), the post-Rome commentaries by pro-family advocates are titled 'The International Criminal Court – World Nightmare' (REAL Women of Canada, 1998a) or 'ICC: Promise of Justice or Threat of Tyranny?' (1998). The latter article states that 'while the ICC could be a wonderful tool for building true justice and freedom everywhere, in the context in which the court has been established and will be used, we fear it will be an extremely powerful weapon in the hands of the international anti-life, anti-family movement'.

The United Nations, although more in some parts than in others, has in recent years explicitly embraced the notion that civil society participation is one of the elements of its legitimacy. A Panel of Eminent Persons has recently been established by the Secretary-General to 'review past and current practices and recommend improvements for the future in order to make the interaction between civil society and the United Nations more meaningful' (*We the Peoples*, 2004). If one believes that there is such a right to participate or interact, and if the United Nations is serious and sincere about being 'open to civil society', it should be open to all civil society representation, not just the kind of representation that is deemed desirable by most delegates. Excluding certain types of groups from participation would infringe on the right to participate. If women's groups have a right to be active at forums such as the ICC negotiations – and they have fought hard for that right – then so do pro-family groups.

Moreover, if one believes that multilateral institutions, however much they may be in need of reform, are still the best place to make international decisions, then it is encouraging, and to be encouraged, that groups who are in principle hostile to such institutions make a strategic decision to participate in multilateral forums and subject themselves to the procedures that prevail there. This, at the same time, should be the criteria for accreditation and participation: it does not matter if pro-family groups would prefer to see the United Nations abolished, or even if they are working actively towards that goal, as long as they play by the rules of the game.

Therefore, any accusations that any kind of group – liberal, conservative, secular, religious, pro-life or pro-choice – is not playing by the rules, such as the accusations of dumping documents in the rubbish levied against some pro-family groups in the ICC case, should be taken extremely seriously. Routine breaking of the rules could undermine the legitimacy of civil society participation as a whole.

While in the first two decades of UN lobbying, the women's movement found adversaries only among states, and could count on the solidarity, or at least neutrality, of fellow NGOs, the presence of pro-family groups at UN forums is now a reality that is not likely to go away. But it is not just a painful reality. The women's movement should recognise that these groups' right to participate in these forums is a logical corollary of their own right to do so. As long as pro-family groups play by the rules, activists in the women's movement should fight them not by putting their energy into vitriolic attacks, but simply by being better – being more present, more energetic, more global, more grassroots, more expert – and should continue to solicit more support from mainstream NGOs. They did so at the ICC negotiations, winning a gender-sensitive Statute, and they can do it again.

6 The missed chance

Banning weapons

Background: three strands of peace movements in the 1990s

Peace movements have a pedigree as long as war. They are also among the oldest and most significant transnational movements of the modern age: 'Peace societies began sprouting in 1815. . . . A renowned International Peace Congress was held in Paris in 1849', the post-Crimean war negotiations in 1856 were influenced by peace activists, and 'by 1900, there were 425 peace societies throughout the world' (Charnovitz, 1997: 192–193). However, they have throughout the past two centuries been so heterogeneous that it is probably correct to speak of loosely connected 'peace movements' than of a single movement. Their roots and orientations have included Christian and non-Christian spiritual pacifism, liberal internationalism, socialism, feminism and anti-imperialism (Carter, 1992: 1–12, 17). In terms of their advocacy activities, they can further be classified into 'those who oppose all wars and by extension all preparations for war; those who oppose a specific type of weapon; those who oppose particular policies relating to arms, and those who protest against a specific war', and finally those who make 'positive attempts to end conflict' (ibid.: 15; see also Van Dungen, 1985: 22–23).

As the peace movements emerged out of the Cold War, they could be divided into three main strands: activism against particular kinds of weapons; activism against specific wars; and activism oriented towards the prevention of war indirectly, through global institution-building and international rule-making. While all three strands were represented at the ICC negotiations, this chapter focuses on activism 'against a particular kind of weapon', which united in the Peace Caucus, and had the most clearly recognisable 'peace profile' in the negotiations.

In the early 1990s, this strand was still dominated by the anti-nuclear movement, which had declined since its heyday in the 1980s but could still command considerable grassroots support. Activities against biological and chemical weapons, on the other hand, have been the almost exclusive remit of a few very specialised NGOs and a handful of academics (Feakes, 2003: esp. 97–100). But while they never had the popular support that activism against nuclear weapons had, they have had more success in codifying prohibitions on these weapons in international law. While chemical weapons had been widely used in the First World War I, all parties vehemently denied this, and acknowledged that the use of such weapons was 'criminal'. In 1925, the prohibition on using chemical and biological weapons was confirmed in the Protocol for the Prohibition of the Use in War of Asphyxiating, Poisonous or Other Gases, and of Bacteriological Methods of Warfare (further: the Gas Protocol). After the Second World War, these bans were strengthened with the Biological Weapons Convention of 1972 and the Chemical Weapons Convention of 1993, which prohibited not just the use, but also the development, production and stockpiling of these weapons (ibid.: 102–106). The anti-nuclear movement, while its size was waning, achieved its biggest legal success in 1996 when the International Court of Justice gave an Advisory Opinion on the use of nuclear weapons. It fell just short of condemning the threat or use of nuclear weapons *per se* under all circumstances, but was unanimous that such use could not be legal unless it was 'compatible with the requirements of international law applicable in armed conflict, particularly those of the principles and rules of humanitarian law, as well as with specific obligations under treaties' (Clark, 2002: 266, quoting the Nuclear Weapons Advisory Opinion). As this chapter shows, it is very difficult to imagine how the use of nuclear weapons could ever be reconciled with the rules and principles of humanitarian law.

But the most successful anti-weapons campaign of the 1990s was undoubtedly the campaign against landmines, culminating in the Landmines Ban Treaty of 1997. The campaign is often mentioned in the same breath as the campaign for an international criminal court, although there was remarkably little connection between the two. However, although the Landmines Ban Treaty has been widely ratified, there are also a number of states, including China, India, Russia and the United States, that have not ratified the treaty, and the prohibition on landmines cannot be considered to have become customary law, as the prohibition on biological and chemical weapons has. More recently, the trade in small arms has received considerable attention with the founding of the International Action Network on Small Arms (IANSA) in August 1998 (IANSA, 1998).

The second strand of peace activism is that of opposition to specific wars. This aspect of peace activism saw sustained global protests during the years of the Vietnam War, and had strong anti-imperialist connections. After Vietnam, the interests of those who remained active spread and shifted to Central America, Palestine, Southern Africa and East Timor. It was transformed during the 1980s and 1990s as the conflicts themselves were affected by the end of the Cold War. The movement was joined by some of those formerly involved in anti-nuclear activism, particularly in Europe, merged with indigenous peace movements, for instance in Israel and the Balkans, and became much more focused on conflict resolution and individual human rights. As the human rights movement itself changed, becoming more focused on impunity and more accepting of the idea of human rights abuses by non-state actors (see also Chapter 2), the worldview and interests of the two movements converged. New international organisations such as Peace Brigades International (founded 1981), International Alert (1985) and the Helsinki Citizens' Assembly (1990) grew out of this new orientation.

Third, a very old but relatively minor part of the peace movement is that which grew out of 'liberal internationalism'. In terms of the classification above, it could be seen as making 'positive contributions to prevent conflict', but at a global scale. It has always 'relied heavily on the role of public opinion and on rational discussion of conflicting interests', and organisations associated with this strand have been strong supporters of international institutions such as the League of Nations, the United Nations and the European Union (Carter, 1992: 3, 10–11). Such organisations, including various world federalist organisations and UN associations, could be classed in today's terminology as 'global governance organisations' (see Chapter 2). They saw a revival in the 1990s, along with the institutions they supported, and they were natural supporters of an international criminal court. One of these organisations, the World Federalist Movement, was in fact the coordinator of the CICC.

A final organisation that should be mentioned in this context is the International Committee of the Red Cross. It is not usually classed as a peace organisation, as it has focused almost from its inception on protecting and assisting victims, rather than opposing war *per se*. But in terms of its mandate of 'promoting and strengthening humanitarian law and universal humanitarian principles' (ICRC website), it could also be considered as belonging to the 'global governance' strand of peace activism, although, as this chapter makes clear, it also advocated on weapons.

There have been moments in history when the various strands of peace movements have pulled together with impressive cohesion and mobilisation. These moments included the campaign against the Vietnam War, against the nuclear arms race in the early 1980s, against the First Gulf War in 1991, and the unprecedentedly large and global mobilisation against the war in Iraq in 2002, when it drew in new constituencies, including Muslims and anti-capitalists. As this chapter will show, the negotiations on the International Criminal Court were definitely not such a moment.

Weapons at the early negotiations

The draft by the International Law Commission did not go into detail on the crimes the ICC would cover, stating merely that they would include genocide, crimes against humanity, war crimes, aggression, and possibly 'treaty crimes', with a list of eligible treaties in an annexe (ILC, 1997: art. 20; Annex). Therefore, it was essentially silent on whether the use of particular weapons could constitute any of these crimes. Nor did the Ad Hoc Committee discuss in any depth the possibility of criminalising weapons.

Early NGO documents by Amnesty International (AI, 1994), the International Commission of Jurists (ICJ, 1995) and Human Rights Watch (1996) included relatively brief sections on definitions of crimes, and made no mention of the use of particular weapons. A later Amnesty International document (AI, 1997) focusing specifically and in great detail on definitions of crimes remained silent on the use of weapons, as did a memorandum by the president of the Yugoslavia tribunal, Antonio Cassese (1996b), on the definition of crimes in the jurisprudence of that tribunal, despite the fact that the tribunal's rules do in fact criminalise 'employment of poisonous or other weapons calculated to cause unnecessary suffering' (HRW, 1998a).

The definition of war crimes, and hence also the inclusion of the use of certain weapons as a war crime, was first seriously discussed in the PrepCom of February 1997, which was open to NGOs (Hall, 1998a: 126). The only civil society document that commented on the use of weapons as war crimes at this time was a paper by the International Committee of the Red Cross. The ICRC was also given the opportunity to address the Preparatory Committee with a speech, in which it proposed that 'to employ weapons, projectiles and material and methods of warfare of a nature to cause superfluous injury or unnecessary suffering, or inherently indiscriminate' should be a war crime in both international and internal conflicts (ICRC, 1997a). This language was derived from the 1899 and 1907 Hague Conventions, a set of fourteen treaties and declarations that formed the first comprehensive codification of humanitarian law. They are now generally considered to have become customary law (Clark, 2002: 263). The 'inherently indiscriminate' phrase was based on the humanitarian law principle that a distinction must be made between the treatment of combatants and civilians, but proved to be more controversial.

Two comprehensive proposals were presented by states on the definition of war crimes. They indicated two different approaches to the weapons issue. The first proposal, by New Zealand and Switzerland, reflected the paper prepared by the Red Cross, including the general criminalisation of weapons 'of a nature to cause superfluous injury or unnecessary suffering, or inherently indiscriminate' (Von Hebel and Robinson, 1999: 106; Clark, 2002: 261). This would leave it to the judges to decide, on the basis of customary law, treaties and jurisprudence, whether any particular weapon would fulfil these criteria. It would have the advantage of flexibility, allowing for new developments in weapons technology as well as in international law, but it would not provide absolute certainty as to what was prohibited and what was not.

The second proposal, presented by the United States, was the outcome of informal discussions with France, the United Kingdom and Japan (Von Hebel and Robinson, 1999: 105–106). It proposed listing as war crimes the use of a particular set of weapons, namely:

- poisonous or poisoned weapons;
- asphyxiating, poisonous or other gases, and all analogous liquids, materials or devices;
- bullets which expand or flatten easily in the human body;
- bacteriological (biological) agents or toxins;
- chemical weapons as defined in the 1993 Convention on Chemical Weapons.

Poisonous weapons and expanding (dumdum) bullets had been prohibited by the Hague Conventions; the language of 'asphyxiating, etc. gases' came from the 1925 Gas Protocol mentioned earlier in the chapter. The same protocol also included 'bacteriological' or biological weapons. The advantage of a specific list, as suggested by this proposal, is the legal certainty it provides. As Roger Clark put it, 'the most important point about those weapons banned *per se* is that it is never lawful to use them. Never, under any circumstances. No considerations of military necessity can ever authorize their use. . . . An absolute rule is just that: absolute' (Clark, 2002: 264). However, the list proposed by the United States excluded a number of more controversial weapons, such as landmines, blinding laser weapons and, above all, nuclear weapons. Syria did propose at this session that the threat or use of nuclear weapons be criminalised, but 'with very little support' (Ware, 1997).

The Weapons Systems Caucus at the PrepComs

The peace groups involved in the ICC process could be classified into the same three categories described above: either they had very broad global governance aims, or they were oriented towards conflict resolution and human rights protection, or they sought the abolition of particular weapons. The first two groups shared many of the aims of the majority of human rights and legal organisations represented at the ICC negotiations, and are therefore not given special attention in this chapter.

The third group founded the Weapons Systems Caucus in late 1997. It aimed to 'make the Statute as restrictive as possible in regard to nuclear weapons, landmines, and other weapons inflicting indiscriminate harm and unnecessary suffering, including blinding laser weapons' (Burroughs and Cabasso, 1999: 470; 'Canada Slammed', 1998). It was later renamed 'Peace Caucus', reflecting the fact that it also wanted to address the issue of aggression, but weapons remained its primary concern (interview Burroughs; Ware, e-mail, 2004b).

It was a small caucus, consisting of nine or ten groups. Its core consisted of nuclear abolitionist groups such as the International Alliance of Lawyers Against Nuclear Arms (IALANA), the Lawyers' Committee on Nuclear Policy and the Western States Legal Foundation. More generally oriented peace and global governance organisations such as the European Law Students Association, the Women's International League for Peace and Freedom, the World Federalist Movement, No Peace Without Justice, PPF Global Alliance (Philippines and Japan) and the United Nations Association of Tamil Nadu were also members of the Caucus (Burroughs and Cabasso, 1999: 470). At least one of its proposals was also supported by a number of domestic organisations from Canada, Norway, Mexico and the United States which were not present at the negotiations, and by the Women's Caucus (Weapons Systems Caucus, 1997).

Conflict resolution and more human rights-oriented peace organisations such as the Carter Center, the Helsinki Citizens' Assembly, International Alert and the Pan-African Reconciliation Council, which were accredited to the conference in Rome, were not part of the Peace

Caucus. This is in line with the new direction such organisations have taken, discussed above. According to CICC coordinator Bill Pace, also the director of the World Federalist Movement, 'The non-anti-nuclear sectors have moved away from the peace community . . . they now go under another umbrella' (interview Pace). Neither was the International Committee of the Red Cross a member – but it generally refrains from joining alliances, so as not to compromise its position of neutrality.

The International Campaign to Ban Landmines was not represented in the ICC negotiating process, and neither were any of the organisations specifically concerned with biological and chemical weapons, although the *CBW Conventions Bulletin* did follow the negotiations from afar ('News Chronology', 1997, 1998a, b).

For the next PrepCom that dealt with definitions of crimes, in December 1997, the Weapons Systems Caucus developed its own proposal. It combined the two earlier proposals, opening with the Red Cross formulation, then '*including, but not limited to*' the five clauses listed by the US proposal, plus two additional clauses: 'threat or use of nuclear weapons' and 'anti-personnel landmines' (Weapons Systems Caucus, 1997). Like the ICRC paper, the Caucus referred extensively to existing international law, including the Hague and Geneva conventions, the just-concluded Landmines Ban Treaty, and the Advisory Opinion of the International Court of Justice on nuclear weapons (ibid.).

The session opened again with the general Red Cross prohibition introduced by New Zealand and Switzerland, and the short, exhaustive US list of prohibited weapons, now proposed by Germany after informal 'NATO' consultations. Canada proposed a compromise solution, adding to the closed list an extra clause prohibiting 'such other weapons or weapons systems as become the subject of a comprehensive prohibition pursuant to customary or conventional international law' (Ware, 1997; Hall, 1998b: 335). According to one source, Canada specifically had landmines in mind in making this proposal ('Canada Slammed', 1998); it was successfully leading the negotiations on the Landmines Ban Convention in the same month. It did not propose an explicit prohibition of landmines, however.

A fourth option emerged, formally submitted by the Philippines, but, according to Alyn Ware of the Weapons Systems Caucus, 'pushed for' by 'Non-Governmental Organizations, which were present in much larger numbers than in February' (Ware, 1997). The text of this option (see Hall, 1998b) was identical to the proposal by the Weapons Systems Caucus, apart from the inclusion of blinding laser weapons, which later also became one of its objectives. This whole text, with all four options in brackets, went to Rome.

On the governmental front, one other relevant development was the adoption by the Non-Aligned Movement (NAM) of a statement that made explicit prohibition of nuclear weapons one of its key objectives for the ICC (Burroughs and Cabasso, 1999: 471). According to Alyn Ware, the Lawyers' Committee on Nuclear Policy was 'vital in getting the CICC into the NAM Summits' (Ware, e-mail, 2004b). However, the credibility of this statement was rather weakened by the fact that leading NAM member India detonated a nuclear bomb on 11 May 1998, to which another member, Pakistan, responded with nuclear tests on 28 and 30 May.

Weapons and the Peace Caucus in Rome

Some of the most comprehensive preparatory documents by NGOs for the Rome conference, including those by Amnesty International and the Lawyers Committee for Human Rights, made no recommendations concerning the weapons clause (AI, 1998a; LCHR, 1998a; Broomhall, 1998). Likewise, the 'Basic Principles', the only joint statement on substance ever to have been published by the Coalition for an International Criminal Court, incorporated concerns on gender, children's rights and victims, but nothing on weapons (CICC, 1998a). Even the Red Cross, in its – brief – opening statement to the Rome conference, did not mention weapons, focusing instead on the independent prosecutor, jurisdiction, and the applicability of the ICC to internal conflict (ICRC, 1998a). An exception was Human Rights Watch, which did devote a few paragraphs to the topic, endorsing the Red Cross variant of a general prohibition (HRW, 1998a).

The now renamed Peace Caucus also issued another position paper, expressing a first preference for the Philippines proposal including both a general prohibition and a non-exclusive list including nuclear weapons, landmines and blinding laser weapons. Its second preference was for the general prohibition only, as formulated by the ICRC. The other two options before the conference – the closed list and the Canadian compromise adding a clause on weapons that will be prohibited in future to this list – it rejected as too restrictive (Peace Caucus, 1998).

In the first week in Rome, delegates from a number of Caribbean and Pacific states and some African, Asian and Middle Eastern states spoke out in favour of either the Red Cross general prohibition or the long list including nuclear weapons, landmines and blinding laser weapons.

Iran, which chaired the NAM meetings, supported this position (Clark, 2002: 269; 'Special Analysis', 1998; Haq, 1998d). The more restrictive proposals were championed not just by France, China and Russia, but also by Denmark and Sweden ('Special Analysis', 1998). A member of the Peace Caucus also specifically criticised Canada for 'missing an opportunity to continue work' on landmines ('Canada Slammed', 1998).

The US ambassador, David Scheffer, characterised inclusion of nuclear weapons, landmines or blinding laser weapons as 'entirely unacceptable . . . a non-starter', and one member of the Peace Caucus acknowledged that 'The United States and NATO will probably have their way' (Haq, 1998d). Indeed, members of the Peace Caucus went to Rome in the belief that there was 'no way' nuclear weapons would be criminalised (interview Burroughs; Ware, e-mail, 2004a). Nonetheless, the Peace Caucus continued to campaign for inclusion of nuclear weapons. According to one Peace Caucus activist,

> [W]e want to avoid the absurd situation whereby the Court would have jurisdiction if someone killed one person with a poisoned arrow or dum-dum bullet, but would not have jurisdiction if the person incinerated a hundred thousand with a nuclear weapon.
> ('Canada Slammed', 1998)

Similarly, John Burroughs of the Lawyers' Committee for Nuclear Policy argued that including biological and chemical weapons under the Statute, while excluding nuclear weapons, would be 'criminalizing the poor man's weapons of mass destruction' ('Nuclear Cloud', 1998). According to members of the Peace Caucus, 'most NGOs were a bit stand-offish' about the weapons issue, fearing that nuclear weapons in particular could wreck the negotiations (interview Burroughs; Ware, e-mail, 2004a).

Among states, India was the most vocal proponent of the inclusion of nuclear weapons as a crime. Others included Samoa and the Philippines (Ware, e-mail, 2004b). However, while India continued to pursue this objective, the unity of the NAM was much weakened at the Rome Conference by the defection of many states to the Like-Minded Group (Benedetti and Washburn, 1999: 31, 33). Like-Minded leaders such as the Scandinavian countries and Canada were disinclined to include nuclear arms or even on landmines because of their controversial status ('Canada Slammed', 1998; 'Special Analysis', 1998): their use is not uncontrovertibly prohibited under international law.

The credibility of India's anti-nuclear stance was, moreover, much weakened by the fact that it had carried out its own nuclear tests only a month earlier. As one journalist wrote rather dramatically,

> Having eaten the forbidden apple of nuclear tests in May, India is now experiencing life in the harsh world outside the garden of Eden. New Delhi's delegates – attending the first global conference since the country associated with the apostle of peace Mahatma Gandhi and the champion of disarmament Jawaharlal Nehru forced its way into the nuclear club – are finding themselves increasingly isolated in the international arena.
>
> (Jaura, 1998)

According to one author, India's position was not necessarily inconsistent, in that it considered possession and testing of nuclear weapons lawful but their actual use illegal (Clark, 2002: 269–270). However, many NGOs and state delegates believed that India's real objective was to 'wreck the Statute', rather than to insert anti-nuclear language (Jaura, 1998; interview Pace; Ware, e-mail, 2004a).

When the first Bureau proposal was presented on 6 July, it included three options: the short US list of weapons, referred to as 'of a nature to cause superfluous injury or unnecessary suffering'; second, the longer list, which included nuclear weapons, landmines and blinding laser weapons, and which included the extra phrase 'inherently indiscriminate'; and finally, the general prohibition, first proposed by the Red Cross, of any weapons 'of a nature to cause superfluous injury or unnecessary suffering, or inherently indiscriminate'. The first two options now included the Canadian final clause listing 'such other weapons and weapons systems as become subject of a comprehensive prohibition', to be determined by the assembly of states parties (Bureau Discussion Paper, war crimes, art. 5 B (o)). Strangely, the weapons clause now only referred to international conflicts, not internal wars (Clark, 2002: 271).

It was becoming clear that a majority of countries were prepared to sacrifice nuclear weapons, with fifty-seven states in favour of option 1, twenty-five for option 2 and just six for option 3 (CICC, 1998b). The next Bureau proposal included only the first option, but with one difference: the 'inherently indiscriminate' phrase from the other two options was included (Bureau Proposal, 1998: art. 5 quarter B (o)), and according to one author, 'the anti-weapons people were told that they had won a great victory' with this (Clark, 2002: 272). Indeed, John Burroughs of the Lawyers' Committee on Nuclear Policy claimed it as a victory, writing, 'the "inherently indiscriminate" language was successfully inserted over the resistance of nuclear weapon states, and should henceforth be used often to describe nuclear weapons' (Burroughs, 1999). But as Clark points out, the phrase is only meaningful within a general prohibition; it has little purpose when it is followed by a specific list of prohibited weapons, excluding nuclear ones.

The struggle to include nuclear weapons was not quite over yet. Iran made a formal proposal on behalf of the NAM to reinstate the prohibition on nuclear weapons ('Fury at Proposal', 1998). However, the African group questioned the unanimity of decision-making in the NAM meeting, and floated the idea of reintroduction of the general prohibition instead, while India continued to push for explicit prohibition of nuclear weapons (Clark, 2002: 278; 'India, a Headache for its Allies', 1998; 'India and US Broadsides Threaten Consensus', 1998). But this was no more than a sideshow, not only in the state negotiations, but also in the attendant civil society lobbying. Weapons were not mentioned in the final appeals by the major players: Amnesty International, Human Rights Watch, the Lawyers Committee for Human Rights, the Women's Caucus or the Red Cross.

However, worse was to come. Some states argued that if nuclear weapons were not expressly included, then biological and chemical weapons, 'poor man's weapons', ought not to be included either. In the last week of the conference, in closed negotiations, the Dutch chair of the working group on nuclear weapons succumbed to this line of argument, reportedly pursued by the Arab states. In what he refers to as a 'Solomonesque' solution, the explicit reference to biological and chemical weapons was deleted, leaving only expanding bullets, poison weapons and 'poisonous gases and analogous materials', relegating all other weapons which might be criminalised to a future annexe, yet to be negotiated (Von Hebel and Robinson, 1999: 116; Burroughs and Cabasso, 1999: 471–472). Such an annexe would be very difficult to negotiate, as it would require the agreement of seven-eighths of all the states parties, and it would not apply to any state that disagreed with the amendment. Furthermore, such an annexe can only list weapons which are already 'the subject of a comprehensive prohibition' under international law, but would nonetheless apply only to those states that agree to the amendment (Clark, 2002: 277).

On the evening of 17 July, India proposed an amendment to the Statute to reinstate the prohibition on nuclear weapons. However, as described above, reopening the negotiations at this point was seen as ruining the prospects for a Statute. The African Group dropped its proposal for a general prohibition and supported the no-action motion by Norway on the Indian amendment, opening the way to adoption of the Statute.

The final Statute, therefore, has just four weapons clauses: poisonous or poisoned weapons; asphyxiating, poisonous or other gases, and all analogous liquids, materials or devices; bullets which expand or flatten easily in the human body; and finally weapons which may be prohibited in the future and listed in an annexe. The second clause, taken from the 1925 Protocol, can be taken to include biological weapons (Feakes, 2003: 103), but the prohibition is not explicit, and does not refer to the 1972 Biological Weapons Convention. Nor is there a reference to the 1993 Chemical Weapons Convention, which is more comprehensive than the 1925 Protocol, prohibiting non-lethal weapons such as tear gas (Perry Robinson, e-mail, 2004).

While no one would suggest that the ICC Statute furthers international law in the area of prohibiting weapons, there is some disagreement on how problematic these provisions are. On the one hand, an international lawyer like Roger Clark (employed as adviser to the Samoan delegation at the ICC negotiations) lambasts the logical absurdity of the weapons clauses, under which 'it is absolutely forbidden to kill someone with a poisoned arrow, and the ICC could have jurisdiction. If, however, one were to incinerate 100,000 people with an atomic weapon, the ICC would have no jurisdiction' (Clark, 2002: 266).

On the other hand, the ICC Statute describes 'murder', 'extermination' and 'other inhumane acts . . . intentionally causing great suffering, or serious injury to body or mental or physical health', carried out as 'part of a widespread or systematic attack directed against any civilian population' as crimes against humanity. 'Wilful killing', 'wilfully causing great suffering, or serious injury to body or mental or physical health' and 'intentionally launching an attack in the knowledge that such an attack will cause incidental loss of life or injury to civilians . . . clearly excessive in relation to the concrete and direct overall military advantage anticipated' are all war crimes. It is difficult to see how biological, chemical or nuclear weapons could be used without breaching these provisions, although it might be possible to use landmines.

Nonetheless, it is fair to say that 'as a forum to consolidate gains made in banishing weapons of a nature to cause superfluous injury or unnecessary suffering, or which are inherently indiscriminate, the Diplomatic Conference was a great disappointment' (Clark, 2002: 279). It is also inescapable to conclude that the Peace Caucus largely failed to achieve its stated objectives.

After Rome

The Rome Conference was followed by the negotiation of a more detailed document entitled 'Elements of Crimes', which gave anti-weapons activists a further opportunity to plead their cause. Human Rights Watch and the ICRC lobbied for the reinsertion of a reference to the 1993 Chemical Weapons Convention, and hence a prohibition of non-lethal gases ('News Chronology', 2000: 25, 28; Perry Robinson, e-mail, 2004). They achieved a footnote that reads 'Nothing in this element shall be interpreted as limiting or prejudicing in any way existing or developing rules of international law with respect to development, production, stockpiling and use of chemical weapons', a strong allusion rather than an explicit reference to the Convention (Elements of Crimes, Article (8) (2) (b) (xviii), n. 48).

There were also some further developments on the anti-nuclear front. Alongside its ratification of the Rome Statute on 9 June 2000, France made an 'interpretative declaration' stating that it considered that nothing in the Rome Statute could 'regulate or prohibit the possible use of nuclear weapons' in the exercise of 'its inherent right of self-defence' (Déclaration Interprétative, 2000). The Lawyers' Committee on Nuclear Policy responded with a statement arguing that nothing supported such an interpretation, and that the rest of the Statute, including for instance criminalisation of attacks on civilians and civilian objects, naturally also applied to nuclear attacks. It further argued that France also continued to be bound by similar provisions in other humanitarian treaties, and that the declaration amounted to a reservation, which the Statute does not allow, and it therefore urged 'states to set forth in a written declaration the unacceptability of the French "interpretation" regarding nuclear weapons' (LCNP, 2000). New Zealand did subsequently make an 'interpretative declaration' of its own on ratifying the Statute. Without making an explicit objection to the French statement, it argues that the scope of article 8 of the ICC Statute, which deals with war crimes, should not be limited to conventional weapons, and that it is irrelevant in this context whether a state is acting in self-defence, citing the International Court of Justice's Advisory Opinion on Nuclear Weapons for support (Interpretative Declaration, 2000).

Conclusion

The Peace Caucus had a difficult mission because its main objective, the explicit criminalisation of nuclear weapons, was 'at odds with the aim of obtaining support or at least tolerance of the Statute from the nuclear weapons states' (Burroughs and Cabasso, 1999: 471). The introduction of an option including landmines and nuclear weapons by the Philippines in December 1997 may have been orchestrated by the Caucus (Ware, 1997), but key members of the Caucus had little illusion that this clause could be maintained (interview Burroughs; Ware, e-mail, 2004a).

In fact, the actual objectives of the Peace Caucus may have been more modest than its stated objectives. According to Alyn Ware, the actual aim was not to get a ban on nuclear weapons into the Statute, but 'to ensure that the NATO States and NWS [Nuclear Weapons States] could not use the omission of such a clause as a legitimisation of their policies' (Ware, e-mail, 2004b). It is difficult to assess whether the Caucus's intent was really so very limited, or whether there is an element of post-hoc rationalisation in this explanation. It does make it clear that, despite the wider official objective, the focus of the Caucus was overwhelmingly nuclear.

The nuclear cause was further hampered by the moral ostracism of India, the state that advocated most vigorously in favour of criminalising nuclear weapons, after the nuclear tests of May 1998. Although some anti-nuclear activists believed there was at least a measure of sincerity in India's position, other civil society activists and state representatives considered it hypocritical, and aimed at wrecking the conference, not at outlawing nuclear weapons.

The Peace Caucus's second option, a general clause prohibiting weapons that are 'inherently indiscriminate' or cause 'unnecessary suffering', was not fulfilled either. While it is impossible to determine with hindsight whether and under what circumstances such a clause might have been maintained, the failure of the Peace Caucus does prompt some reflection concerning the dynamics within the civil society community involved in the ICC.

For the NGO Coalition and most of its participants, weapons of mass destruction were an avoided topic, because they were more interested in human rights issues, and because it was seen as a potential conference wrecker (Burroughs and Cabasso, 1999: 474). The Peace Caucus might have tried harder to lobby within the Coalition itself. It might, for instance, have pushed its second-best position of a general prohibition clause as supported by the Red Cross as an acceptable compromise to be supported by a wider constituency. But the CICC had no mechanisms for mediating the interests of its different members: 'there was no thorough discussion, still less any formal decision-making, among all participating NGOs' (ibid.: 474). The loose structure of the

CICC was mostly seen as an asset, but it meant for instance that the rather marginal Peace Caucus groups were not in on the adoption of the Coalition's 'Basic Principles' just before the Rome conference, a rather hastily assembled document reflecting the concerns of members of the CICC's Steering Group. They incorporate concerns on gender, children's rights and victims, but nothing on weapons of mass destruction.

On the other hand, anti-weapons activists themselves bear some responsibility for the disappearance of the clauses on landmines and on biological and chemical weapons. An appearance by the International Coalition to Ban Landmines (ICBL) might have shamed the chairing country, Canada, into championing a prohibition on at least the use of anti-personnel mines: the Rome conference took place just six months after the successful conclusion of the Ottawa Convention to Ban Landmines, and the award of the Nobel Prize to ICBL. The Peace Caucus included members of ICBL, and had officially made criminalisation of the use of landmines one of its objectives, but it did not run a high-profile campaign on the issue, as its core members were focused on nuclear weapons. Nor did activists more centrally involved in the landmines ban campaign join the negotiations, despite having been invited to do so by the Peace Caucus (Ware, e-mail, 2004b).

With respect to biological and chemical weapons, the responsibility of the Peace Caucus goes further. According to various reports, it was the Arab states that particularly insisted on the exclusion of biological and chemical weapons (Clark, 2002: 274; Burroughs, 1999). It is not clear why their objections should hold such sway, since it was clear even at the time that, with the exception of Jordan, they were not likely to ratify the Statute (and at the time of writing, none but Jordan has ratified). Arab objections on other issues, such as exclusion of the death penalty or the use of the term 'gender', were generally overruled. The argument by the Canadian negotiators that 'excluding nuclear weapons while including chemical and biological weapons was . . . impossible, since a great many delegations believed that to include the latter would have sent a political signal that the former were more acceptable' (Kirsch and Holmes, 1999: 31) does not hold water. Whatever one may think of the acceptability of one or the other morally, the ICC Statute was meant to codify existing international law, and the use of biological and chemical weapons has been much more unambiguously prohibited under international law than the use of nuclear weapons. Their prohibition was acknowledged as customary law as early as 1925. A more plausible explanation is that the concession to the Arab states could safely be granted because no one, either among states or in civil society, was making much of a case for them.

The anti-biological and chemical weapons community appears to have been largely unaware of the ICC negotiations until after the conference: 'Few if any of the civil society actors in CB disarmament paid much attention to the negotiation of the ICC Statute and none were in Rome for the final negotiations' (Feakes, 2003: 106).

Meanwhile, the Peace Caucus, in its quixotic attempt to have nuclear weapons criminalised, made the argument that prohibiting biological and chemical weapons, but not nuclear ones, amounted to 'criminalizing the poor man's weapons of mass destruction' ('Nuclear Cloud', 1998). The same argument was made by the Arab states, and, as already stated, accepted by the Bureau drafting the final version of the Statute.

This chapter describes the failure of attempts to criminalise the use of particular weapons under the ICC, including nuclear weapons, landmines, and more comprehensive and up-to-date references to biological and chemical weapons. While the chances of criminalising nuclear weapons were never very promising, the anti-weapons advocacy as a whole was also hampered by a lack of solidarity and cohesion within global civil society. This deficiency operated on two levels: between the civil society mainstream and the anti-nuclear activists involved in the ICC negotiations; and between the latter and the wider disarmament community, including anti-biological and chemical weapons and anti-landmine campaigners.

The major players in the Coalition for an International Criminal Court, which included mainly human rights organisations, but also the coordinating organisation, the World Federalist Movement, were cautious about nuclear weapons, while being quite prepared to take radical or utopian positions on other issues, such as for instance universal jurisdiction (see Chapter 4). They were largely silent on other weapons. The same was true for peace groups with more of a conflict resolution or global governance than a weapons orientation. Even the ICRC abandoned its weapons advocacy in favour of other priorities during the Rome conference. The Peace Caucus, while broadly supportive of the other objectives of the CICC (interview Pace; Ware, e-mail, 2004b), was marginalised in its nuclear weapons advocacy.

Second, there was no close cooperation between the different anti-weapons constituencies. Owing to this fragmentation, the Peace Caucus was dominated by anti-nuclear groups, and civil society actors on biological and chemical weapons and on landmines, who actually had more to lose or gain from the ICC negotiations but were apparently not sufficiently aware of their significance, were absent. A more balanced peace caucus might have made a stronger case for the general prohibition as advocated by the ICRC, and a stronger connection with other peace constituencies in the CICC. Moreover, rather than jealously guarding the language on biological and chemical weapons, the Peace Caucus may actually have contributed to the weakening of these provisions because of its nuclear focus.

Like the issue of gender, but in a more subtle manifestation, this chapter has demonstrated that global civil society should not be considered a consistent moral force. On the contrary, even ostensibly coherent civil society communities like the Coalition for an International Criminal Court, or the peace movement, can suffer from fragmentation and internal contradictions.

7 A global civil society achievement

Why rejoice?

What was achieved

The first achievement of global civil society with respect to the Statute for an International Criminal Court is that there should be such a Statute, and Court, at all. As discussed in Chapter 1, the idea was first invented in civil society, and was kept alive, developed and advocated in international legal associations for 125 years. Even a few years before the adoption of the Statute, CICC coordinator Bill Pace was told by a leading expert in international affairs to '"keep working on this, but don't get your hopes up too high for it isn't going to happen in your lifetime, or your children's lifetime, or your grandchildren's lifetime"' (Pace, 1999: 193). Secretary-General Kofi Annan, too, emphasised in his ceremonial speech at the adoption of the Statute that it was 'an achievement which, only a few years ago, nobody would have thought possible' (Annan, 1998).

In terms of the content of the Statute, undoubtedly the most important achievement was the prosecutor's authority to choose his or her own cases (see Chapter 3). By the admission of the key diplomats involved, this could not have been achieved without sustained and overwhelming NGO pressure. Beyond NGOs, the active involvement of the prosecutors of the Yugoslavia and Rwanda tribunals was another key factor in legitimising the idea of an independent prosecutor. Within a few years, global civil society succeeded, first, in persuading states that independent authority of the prosecutor was desirable, and second, in persuading them that it was achievable because they wanted it.

While, as discussed in Chapter 4, the jurisdiction regime of the ICC is problematic, the fact that states automatically accept the Court's full jurisdiction for all the crimes in the Statute when they ratify it is another achievement. It is a great advance over the 'à la carte' jurisdiction regime originally proposed. Automatic jurisdiction was the consistent and unanimous position of civil society actors, and, like the principle of an independent prosecutor, gradually came to be accepted by states. The only provision that detracts from the achievement is a temporary loophole on war crimes, but so far this has only been taken advantage of by two states.

Largely as a result of the advocacy of a very large, active and expert civil society Women's Caucus, the Statute of the Court marks a great advance in the gender sensitiveness of international law. In terms of crimes, it includes a comprehensive definition of gender-based war crimes and crimes against humanity, a gender dimension to the definition of slavery, and the inclusion of persecution on the basis of gender as a component of crimes against humanity. Other provisions include references to the gender balance and gender-specific expertise of the judges and other staff of the Court; a reference to gender in a general non-discrimination clause; and protection for and gender-sensitive treatment of victims and witnesses. On the other hand, partly as a result of pressure from 'pro-family' groups, definitions of the term 'gender' itself, and of 'forced pregnancy', were forged in such a way that they should not be an obstacle to any state's ratification of the Statute, regardless of its general gender policies (see Chapter 5).

Intense pressure from civil society prevented war crimes committed in internal conflict situations from being excluded from the Statute. A special 'Victims' Rights Group' played an important role in forging rules that balance the need for fair and effective prosecutions against the protection, sensitive treatment and rights of victims and witnesses. The 'Child Rights Caucus' played a role in the criminalisation of conscription of children under 15, a new element in humanitarian law.

Many state representatives in the ICC negotiations, including the successive chairs Bos and Kirsch, have remarked on, and praised, the strong involvement and indeed influence of global civil society in the process of negotiating the Statute for an International Criminal Court (Bos, 1999: 45; Kirsch and Holmes, 1999: 11, 37). Perhaps the strongest expression of this sentiment came from a diplomat who did not belong to the Like-Minded Group, Israeli Chief Counsel Alan Baker: 'In all my years of international work, I've never seen the NGOs play a more powerful role. . . . They were in on nearly every meeting. They were in on everything' (*Wall Street Journal* quoted in Pace, 1999: 201).

Why let global civil society in? The democratic deficit

As this book shows, the influence of global civil society actors on the Statute is undeniable. But why should state representatives be so pleased to be sharing the stage with new actors whose mandate to be part of the negotiations is much less obvious than their own? Should we share their enthusiasm?

According to Adriaan Bos, the Dutch chair of the ICC negotiations until Rome, global civil society involvement 'fills in gaps arising from a democratic deficit in the international decision-making process' (1999: 44–45). Although international law-making has not traditionally been a democratic process, there is an increasing sense among national and international diplomats that, as more decisions have moved up to the international level, international decision-making, and international law-making in particular, ought to be (more) democratic.

This idea is related to a more general recognition by political thinkers that, while more states have been converted to parliamentary democracy, the onset of globalisation has eroded the substance of democratic participation and choice (see, for instance, Held, 1995; McGrew, 1997; Scholte, 2001; Anderson, 2000). The enthusiasm for global civil society, and the claim that it makes international decision-making 'more democratic', should probably be seen in this context. But does it make international decision-making more democratic? This chapter assesses this claim with respect to the global civil society involvement in the ICC negotiations.

This assessment requires, first of all, a brief inquiry into the meaning of democracy. Its Greek root means simply 'rule by the people', but in its modern use the term usually implies a system of governance whereby 'the people' periodically elect representatives, while key civil and political rights are observed. It is difficult to make a direct link between either of these meanings and the contribution of global civil society to international decision-making processes such as the ICC negotiations. In fact, Kenneth Anderson's strong objection to the idea of a global civil society is based precisely on what he believes to be a conflation between the role of elected representatives at the national level and NGOs at the global level. 'But who elected the international NGOs?', he asks, and goes on to observe that most NGOs are 'not very often connected, in any direct way, to masses of "people"' (Anderson, 2000: 112–118).

This is true. But neither, many democratic theorists would point out, are political parties. Since the 1970s, there has been a severe drop in the number of party members, attendance at party conferences, and voter turn-out in most established democracies. Like the electorate at large, democratic theorists became increasingly disillusioned with representative democracy, calling it 'thin' or 'procedural' democracy. While by and large continuing to advocate representation and civil and political rights as minimum conditions for democracy, they explored forms that would make citizens participate more actively in politics. They referred to such forms as strong (Barber, 1984), participatory (Pateman, 1970) and, especially, as deliberative (Bessette, 1980; Cohen and Rogers, 1983; Gutmann and Thompson, 1996) democracy.

It is on such notions of democracy, rather than on classic representation, that the argument is built that global civil society democratises international decision-making, or 'global governance', as its proponents tend to call it. They agree that such processes are not democratic in their present form, but contend that global civil society participation makes them more so than they would otherwise be (Scholte, 2001; Van Rooy, 2004). Global civil society has been conceptualised as a 'functional equivalent' (Rosenau, 1998: 40–41) or 'alternative mechanism' (Scholte, 2001: 15) to the multi-party representational system, for democratising global governance.

The next section examines some of these supposed democratic functions of global civil society in the light of this study on the ICC Statute: contributions to transparency, equality and deliberation. The subsequent section revisits the remaining problem areas, representation and participation, again in the light of the ICC negotiations, reassesses to what extent global civil society does democratise international decision-making processes, and also makes some recommendations regarding increased participation. The fourth section suggests that the tortured democracy question is not the only justification for global civil society involvement in international fora. It discusses the much-overlooked and by no means unproblematic 'ethical contribution' of global civil society and offers a qualified defence of more international law, with more global civil society participation, on this basis.

Democratising contributions

Transparency

Transparency or openness is a necessary condition of all forms of democracy. Whether in direct or representative democracy, the process of deliberation and the eventual vote must take place openly. Even in experimental forms of democratic procedure that eschew the vote, public discussion is highly valued. Karl Popper (1952) considered 'openness' the prime instrument to keep any form of government from usurping too much power. More recently, Gutmann and Thompson have drawn on such different philosophers as Jeremy Bentham and Immanuel Kant to construct publicity as a necessary condition for deliberative democracy, while also insisting (in line with human rights law) that certain forms of regulated secrecy are necessary in a democratic society (Gutmann and Thompson, 1996: 95–127).

Yet in international negotiations, secrecy has traditionally been the norm. All that became available to the public was the final product – sometimes. There were also secret treaties such as the infamous Molotov–Von Ribbentrop pact. This changed somewhat with the advent of superpower summits and international UN conferences after the Second World War. Now, citizens would be informed via the media that negotiations were proceeding, politicians might make statements, and journalists would speculate about the outcome.

Nonetheless, the substance of the negotiations would still take place behind closed doors. Global civil society coalitions have really changed this, and the Coalition for an International Criminal Court is a prime example. Its working methods (as described in Chapter 2) included forming twelve shadow teams to monitor negotiations on different parts of the Statute, debriefing friendly state delegates after closed meetings, and keeping 'virtual vote' tallies on crucial issues. These mechanisms made the official decision-making process much more transparent: for its members, for journalists and, through them, for a wider interested audience and even for state delegates. The entire texts of interim proposals, with an analysis, were reprinted in one of the special conference newspapers. Information was also sent to thousands of national activists and interested observers by the Coalition itself, by some of its member NGOs, and by the press teams of two special news bulletins devoted to the conference's proceedings. The CICC took the potential for making international negotiations transparent to its limits, and in turn used this publicity as leverage on states: 'Show the governments in Rome that the world is watching', wrote Rik Panganiban, editor of the Coalition's publication, four weeks into the Rome conference; 'Email to us in Rome your messages for your government or for all governments, and we will try to publish as many as we can in the CICC Monitor' (Panganiban, 1998).

The fact that the final conference took place at a UN building in Rome with which most delegates were unfamiliar, the building of the Food and Agriculture Organization, contributed to this transparency, making it very difficult for them to slink off into remote rooms for secret meetings (interview Donat-Cattin).

More importantly, perhaps, many state representatives found these channels of publicity useful, to state their position or vent their frustration with other states or with the process of negotiation, in particular when they believed that public opinion might be on their side. An article in *On the Record*, for instance, records in detail on the proceedings of a closed meeting, where 'according to one report', twenty-seven of the twenty-nine delegates objected to the British chair's proposal, 'a growing number of delegates' felt that Britain was a stalking horse for the United States, and one 'Scandinavian delegate' is directly quoted venting frustration with the British position ('British Allies, NGOs Furious', 1998). As the conference wore on, state delegates began to complain in the media about the lack of transparency of the process itself ('Chairman Struggles', 1998; 'Where Are Decision Being Made?', 1998). This is an interesting development, because state delegates thus addressed the interested wider public with an appeal to a norm of transparency which has no tradition in international negotiations.

Moreover, there seems to be a relation between the extent of transparency of negotiations and their final outcome. In the two instances described in this book in which final decisions were made in great secrecy, the outcomes were unsatisfactory to civil society actors: this applies to the jurisdiction regime as well as the omission of an explicit reference to biological weapons.

The first of these cases is particularly interesting, because it is one of the very few instances in the ICC negotiations where the express preferences of the majority of states were overridden in favour of the preferences of a very few 'powerful' states (see Chapter 4). The few Like-Minded states that were in on this secretive negotiation process chose not to go the route of publicity and appeal to public opinion, and suffered defeat. After the fact, a German delegate did write an article exposing exactly what had happened and defending his government's record to the readers of the *European Journal of Crime, Criminal Law and Criminal Justice* (Kaul, 1998).

Before and after the five frenetic weeks of the Rome conference, the public education aspect played a larger role than publicising the exact proceedings in the negotiations: explaining plainly in local languages what the International Criminal Court was, and why it should matter, for the benefit of a wider audience. In this respect, the ICC case typifies a more general strength of global civil society: with respect to rather esoteric topics like global warming, Third World debt or intellectual property rights, it opens up more general debates, in which active citizens can inform themselves and take part.

As in national democracies, certain discussions and negotiations will continue to take place behind closed doors, but global civil society has been shown to play an important role in shifting the balance much further towards openness as the default setting in international negotiations.

Levelling the playing field

Another key condition of democracy, representative or deliberative, is equality. According to David Beetham, 'a system of collective decision-making can be said to be democratic to the extent that it is subject to control by all members of the relevant association, or all those under its authority, considered as equals' (1999: 5). Formally, there is such equality between the members of the association called the United Nations, at least in its General Assembly and Economic and Social Council, if not in the Security Council. The ICC negotiations followed the General Assembly model in this respect: all states had an equal right to speak, and an equal vote. However, in practice some states are of course more equal than others. This is a question not just of perceived power, but also of capacity to be involved in multiple complex negotiations. Regardless of whether one believes that citizens should somehow be able to have a direct involvement in global processed that affect them, levelling the playing field between the formally equal players, the states, would contribute to democratising international decision-making. Global civil society does at times play such a role. Most eye-catching has probably been the expert advice, and publicity, given to developing countries in the negotiations of the World Trade Organization (WTO) in recent years (Said and Desai, 2003: 80–82).

In the ICC negotiations, civil society made various contributions to empowering smaller and poorer states in the process, and giving them a more equal footing with traditionally powerful states (see Chapter 2). The documents produced by individuals and NGOs helped to educate them with respect to the issues involved. The provision of interns and legal experts swelled their delegations in quality and quantity. The monitoring, by the NGOs, of both public and, as far as possible, secret negotiations, in terms both of the substance of the debate and of the numbers in favour of certain positions, made the process more transparent and easier to follow for such states.

But its method of recording the 'virtual vote', discussed extensively in this book, was perhaps the most important, as it focused attention on absolute numbers of states in favour of particular positions. Without this effort, the fact that, for instance, more than 80 per cent of the states favoured an independent prosecutor would simply have gone unrecorded. Now it became a topic of debate and a counterweight to the inevitable spotlight on the position of 'important' states such as the five permanent members of the Security Council. Thus, the formal equality of states was given a little more substance by at least polling and publicising each state's views, in circumstances where actual voting was avoided except at the very end.

Deliberation

The idea of deliberative democracy is that proposals can be debated on their merits through rational arguments rather than solely on the basis of representation of interests. This aspect of democracy is therefore related to the ethical contribution discussed below. There are two components to this question: whether global civil society made the official state debates more deliberative and less focused on narrow interests, and whether there was a form of deliberative decision-making going on within global civil society. On the first count, the answer is clearly 'yes'. As discussed in Chapter 2, numerous conferences, seminars and unofficial retreats were organised, not just all over Europe, but in Trinidad, in India, in Sierra Leone, in South Africa, etc. There is no doubt that the numerous conferences and seminars, the Sicilian retreats, academic articles and NGO position papers, contributed to a global, albeit specialist, debate on the merits of the international criminal court, which informed and influenced the ultimate decision-making by state delegates.

Moreover, deliberative democracy entails giving and demanding reasons for each position, reasons that would, at least theoretically, be capable of swaying other participants in the debate. It also means participants should to some extent be prepared to be swayed by arguments that appear 'reasonable'. This disposition on the part of states, fostered by the constant discussions with civil society representatives, clearly played a role in the negotiations over the independent prosecutor. When states expressed reasonable fears that the independent prosecutor could be overzealous if unrestrained, a reasonable proposal was made that all prosecutions should be subject to the permission of a pre-trial chamber. When states expressed reasonable concern that the Security Council's mandate on peace and security would be hindered by prosecutions that might, for instance, upset peace negotiations, a reasonable proposal was made to give the Security Council an 'inverted veto' (see Chapter 3). In the atmosphere created among other things by the presence of the former prosecutors Goldstone and Arbour, assertions of naked interest seemed simply inappropriate, and the United States in particular did make every effort to argue its position. The 'reasonable solutions' to meet ostensible objections therefore made it difficult to continue to object to the independent prosecutor – and in fact the United States has based subsequent objections to the Court on the jurisdiction regime, not the prosecutor.

On the second count, of internal deliberation, there is rather more doubt. The NGO Coalition for an International Criminal Court was inclusive and tolerant in principle and in practice. A very wide range of groups that supported the broad goal of a 'just, effective and independent court' joined the Coalition. This included even the small minority of 'family-oriented' groups that were opposed to the aims of the Women's Caucus, unless it became clear that they were generally hostile to the idea of a strong Court. They were met with irritation by most NGOs and many state delegates, but tolerated, accredited, and given access to the same facilities as others (interviews Pace, Hall Martinez; Facio, 1998: 5).

However, it must also be said that the Coalition did not favour extensive internal deliberation. As Burroughs and Cabasso (1999: 474) write,

> [T]here was no thorough debate, still less any formal collective decision-making, among all participating NGOs. Partly this was for practical reasons, because of the number of NGOs, the cumbersome internal decision-making procedures of some NGOs, and the onslaught of events, and partly because it was deemed too divisive to get into controversial matters. Partly, too, the NGO Coalition lacked the kind of culture of consensus reflecting commitments to social transformation, non-violence, and representation of popular demands.

The Coalition emphasised pluralism rather than internal democracy and chose to take few common positions. The Steering Committee, and the coordinator in particular, had good reasons for such an approach, having 'experienced the break-downs and break-ups of NGO steering committees' all too often, and it was a matter of 'amazing grace' that this Coalition survived such pressures (Pace, 1999: 208). However, the few common positions taken, and even informal understandings about the priorities, were crucial, as leading state delegates often channelled their consultation with NGOs through the Coalition (interview Bos).

These positions, or non-positions, did not come about through genuine deliberation among all or most members of the Coalition, and it must be said that, in terms of internal deliberative democracy, the Coalition was wanting. Unlike Burroughs and Cabasso, I would argue that this lack was caused not by a lack of a 'culture of consensus', but, on the contrary, by an unspoken assumption that there was, and ought to be, a consensus.

There certainly appears to have been such an assumption on the part of some government officials. As the Dutch chair put it, 'I was delighted with the way the Coalition succeeded in making all the NGO interests into a coherent unity, as I saw the importance of involving them, but I could not consult with every individual NGO' (interview Bos; translation mine). In its recent report, the Panel of Eminent Persons on United Nations–Civil Society Relations expresses a similar desire for neat amalgamation of civil society views through 'disciplined networking and peer review processes of the constituencies' (*We the Peoples*, 2004: para. 26).

Alison Van Rooy goes even further in her recent book, suggesting – although not ultimately defending – the idea not only that a united front makes civil society campaigning more effective, but that a lack of it detracts from the moral authority of civil society: 'The rule here suggests that if activists cannot agree on a united position, there are fewer reasons to listen to what they have to say' (2004: 99).

But is such unity really the most desirable in terms of fostering deliberation? As Iris Marion Young puts it, deliberative democracy should not be 'a comfortable place of conversation among those who share language, assumptions, and ways of looking at issues' (1997: 401). On the contrary, 'Confrontation with different perspectives, interests, and cultural meanings teaches individuals the partiality of their own, and reveals to them their own experience as perspectival' and 'While not abandoning their own perspectives, people who listen across differences come to understand something about the ways that proposals and policies affect others differently situated' (ibid.: 403).

While precisely playing that role of bringing the experience of 'others' to the attention of state representatives, the CICC did perhaps too much resemble a 'comfortable place of conversation', and fell into the trap of providing a convenient single 'civil society perspective' to the United Nations and state officials, instead of reflecting a sometimes confusing, sometimes confrontational plurality of voices. While in the case of the ICC this does not seem to have detracted at all from its effectiveness, such lack of space and time for open and free deliberation can have consequences for the legitimacy as well as the creativity of global civil society, and hence for its influence, in the long term.

On the other hand, the confrontation between the women's groups and pro-family groups described in Chapter 5 does not meet the requirements of 'deliberative democracy' either, as listening to one another and engaging in a rational set of arguments and counterarguments is also one of the characteristics of the idea of deliberation, and there was certainly no such listening process between these two types of groups. Nonetheless, one could argue that the presence of both perspectives contributed to the deliberative process of the negotiations as a whole. Certainly the resolution of the fraught issues of forced pregnancy and the definition of gender (Chapter 5) can be considered textbook examples of a beneficial compromise outcome of a deliberative process.

If the United Nations is serious about the role of global civil society as fostering real deliberative processes, it should actively look for a *plurality* of civil society views, including starkly opposing ones, instead of trying to weed out such controversy before allowing civil society entry into its chambers. The ICC case has shown that networks are a powerful tool in strengthening the potential influence of global civil society on state negotiations. However, it has also shown that they have a tendency to homogenise views, neglect minority views and of course exclude views that oppose their founding mission. Therefore, a heavy focus on networks is not conducive to the role of global civil society as fostering reasoned debate between different views.

This section has shown that global civil society can, as it has in the case of the ICC, contribute to the transparency of international negotiation processes, to greater equality of the participant states, and to deliberative debate. But is this enough for us to conclude that global civil society democratises processes of international decision-making? The next section examines two further key areas that are considerably more problematic: representation and participation.

Voice, not vote: representation and participation

Representation

Representative democracy was invented because the decision-making constituencies, the *demos*, of nation-states were too large and too dispersed to allow every individual to take part in debates and voting. It is therefore natural that, when thinking about the possibility of a global democracy, or democratising existing global institutions, representative mechanisms of democracy spring to mind. Some would argue that the UN General Assembly already functions as such: now that three-quarters of the world's states are at least formally democratic, one could argue that citizens elect their governments, and the governments represent them in the United Nations.

However, there are various problems with this line of thinking: governments, unlike parliaments, are only formed out of the winning party or parties. The General Assembly is therefore not comparable to national parliaments, because only the national 'winners' are represented. Moreover, complex international issues are not usually an important element in election campaigns. The ICC was not a major issue in any national election campaign. The fact that it even appeared in the Labour Party manifesto in the United Kingdom in 1997 was an anomaly. We still elect national governments primarily to govern us, not to represent us at the international level. So, as is often remarked, the United Nations does not, in fact, represent 'We the peoples', but 'We the governments'.

So, can global civil society represent 'We the peoples' instead? The Panel on UN–civil society relations certainly seems to suggest this by calling its report *We the Peoples: Civil Society, the United Nations and Global Governance* (2004). But how does this representation work? Some organisations have a mass membership. Amnesty International is considered a very large NGO, with more than 1.8 million members from 150 countries (AI website), but this is nothing compared to the 148 million combined membership of the ICFTU family of trade unions (ICFTU website). Other influential organisations such as Greenpeace, Oxfam or WWF (formerly the World Wide Fund for Nature) do not have members, just financial 'supporters' – although Greenpeace does claim to speak for its 2.8 million supporters (Greenpeace website). As Van Rooy has pointed out, the geographical spread and depth of commitment of members differ vastly between organisations, as do procedures for internal democracy (2004: 62–76). There are also very small organisations, and in the negotiations on the International Criminal Court as elsewhere, there were many civil society actors that did not claim to represent anyone but themselves.

It becomes obvious very quickly that conceptualising global civil society as a global equivalent of political parties, organising the global electorate into voting blocs whom they represent in international negotiations, is inaccurate and misleading. Having a large membership base may be a source of legitimacy and influence for particular organisations, but democratic representation in the traditional sense cannot be considered a functioning attribute of global civil society.

But are there other forms of representation? And who or what ought to be represented? David Held (2002) uses the phrase 'overlapping communities of fate' to express the fact that those who are affected by certain decisions are, owing to globalisation, no longer always found neatly in a single political entity, controlled by a democratic process. Global civil society can sometimes be a solution to such situations where the decision-making is not where the voting is, through an informal form of representation. One could argue, for instance, that global civil society represented people in developing countries living with HIV/AIDS in its advocacy on the production of generic drugs surrounding the WTO negotiations on intellectual property. In the absence of any other form of representation, this may be helpful to those affected, and can certainly be argued to have been helpful in the example given.

But the fact that there is no agreed form for consulting those who are supposedly represented remains problematic. In the case of the Narmada dam, for instance, it has been argued that there was representation at the international level of those Indian villagers who opposed the dam, but no such representation of those who would benefit from it.

But who would constitute the 'community of fate' for the ICC negotiations? Who is affected, and should therefore be represented? Negotiation of such general rules of international law may affect all our futures, but it is impossible to pinpoint in advance exactly who will be affected, and how. Representation should therefore be conceptualised in a very different way in these situations. Global civil society can still make claims 'on behalf of', but claims on behalf of future victims of human rights violations, on behalf of the environment or on behalf of the unborn child have little or nothing to do with a parliamentarian's work on behalf of his or her constituency. On the one hand, consultation mechanisms are not a necessary part of such claims. On the other hand, no formal voting rights can or should be based on it. Global civil society is not, and should not be, seen as a kind of global parliament. Or, as Mike Edwards puts it, civil society is 'a voice not a vote' (2003).

Participation

Another way of conceptualising this is to say that participation, not representation, is the point of global civil society. As the Panel on UN–Civil Society Relations puts it, 'citizens increasingly act politically by participating directly, through civil society mechanisms, in policy debates that particularly interest them. This constitutes a broadening from representative to participatory democracy' (*We the People*, Executive Summary: x) But whose voices are, and should be, heard under the banner of global civil society? Who gets to participate?

Some actors, it should be said, do not wish to participate, or at least not on the invitation and according to the rules of the decision-makers. As Iris Marion Young puts it, they typically 'make public noise outside while deliberation is supposedly taking place on the inside', although sometimes they 'invade the houses of deliberation and disrupt their business' (2001: 673). As described in Chapter 2, the ICC negotiations saw a few such global civil society actors, such as the anti-capitalist Zapatista solidarity group Ya Basta, which demanded the indictment of Mexican president Zedillo ('Indict Zedillo First', 1998), and the Mothers of the Plaza de Mayo, who disrupted the speech of the Argentinian Justice Minister ('Madres Thrown Out', 1998).

In fact, the differences between the Madres de la Plaza de Mayo and the Abuelas (grandmothers) de la Plaza de Mayo, both present at the ICC negotiations in Rome, typify the differences between 'outsider' and insider' activism. The Abuelas go through the courts in their efforts to find the children of their disappeared children and see the perpetrators punished. Through their efforts, Argentinian junta leader Jorge Videla was reimprisoned in 1997 (Kirk, 1998a). Their president, Estela Barnes de Carlotto, came to the ICC negotiations in order to have forced disappearances included in the Statute as a crime against humanity (Jackson, 1998a). The Madres 'think that accepting financial compensation and exhumation of bodies are a "betrayal" for their children – because this, in a legal sense, stops what had been an ongoing crime' (Kirk, 1998a). While there was some debate in the ICC negotiations on recognising past disappearances as an ongoing crime, the Madres did not have any faith in the negotiations, and preferred to disrupt them instead.

But as Young points out, such outsiders do in fact 'aim to communicate specific ideas to a wide public' (2001: 676). In this particular case, they attracted media attention to what they considered the inadequacy of the ICC negotiations, which accepted the participation of the – in their eyes illegitimate – Argentinian and Mexican governments, and would not consider past disappearances as part of its agenda. One could argue that such actors do in fact participate in the process, if only from the outside and on their own terms.

Another group that was largely absent from the civil society scene was those conservatives or sovereignists who are sceptical and suspicious of international institutions such as the ICC. Undoubtedly there is also such a constituency in civil society, in the United States but also elsewhere. But it did not mobilise to prevent the establishment of the Court – or rather, it did not do so at the site of negotiations. The only manifestation of such groups was in relation to 'gender clauses', but it is clear from the documents, websites and newsletters of these groups that their misgivings about the Court went beyond gender alone. The subsequent 'war on the Court' by the Bush administration, which also formed part of the 2004 re-election campaign, has made it clear that such views are not irrelevant, however.

As is argued in Chapter 5, the United Nations and the civil society groups themselves should not attempt to exclude such 'nasty views' from their deliberations. On the contrary, procedures to invite and manage different and even opposing perspectives should be improved. This is a requirement for having serious deliberation, it is necessary in order to approach more closely the ideal of free and equal participation, and finally it should in fact be considered a victory for the United Nations and for multilateralism if such groups do devote energy to participating in its debates, rather than fighting the organisation from the outside.

Thus far, I have discussed groups and individuals who were either just outside the gates or entirely absent by choice. But what of those who cannot participate? There was one indication – although accounts differ – that an NGO briefing involving a Chinese paediatrician and the French parents of two child AIDS victims was blocked by China and France ('China and France Shut the Door', 1998; 'China Scuttles NGO Meet', 1998). Such deliberate blockings, which were particularly characteristic of the 1995 Beijing Conference on Women, have become rarer, as the furore they cause tends to result in negative publicity for the state, and more publicity for the civil society organisation and its cause than they might otherwise receive. Nonetheless, states still have the power to block accreditation to the United Nations' Economic and Social Council. During the Cold War, states would routinely deny accreditation to organisations they labelled either 'communist' or 'imperialist'. While such practices receded in the 1990s, today there is a new label: 'terrorist'. As is discussed in Chapter 2, giving the accreditation process over to one of the civil society actors themselves, as was done in the ICC case, is not the solution. But neither is leaving it in the hands of states conducive to wide participation. The recommendation of the UN Panel (*We the Peoples*, 2004: 54–56) to give the UN secretariat a greater role in deciding on accreditation is to be welcomed, although it is on the conservative side, still allowing for state vetoes, although not by a single state.

Beyond deliberate obstruction by states, there is a wider problem with participation. The UN Panel describes participatory democracy as a process in which 'anyone can enter the debates that most interest them, through advocacy, protest, and in other ways' (*We the Peoples*,

2004: para. 13). But a few pages later it acknowledges that there are practical constraints: 'if the United Nations brought everyone relevant into each debate, it would have endless meetings without conclusion' (para. 23). As Ricardo Blaug puts it wryly,

> Whether due to there being simply too many of us, to the excessive complexity and interdependence of the problems we face, to a perceived inefficiency of deliberation, or to a perceived lack of ability and motivation on the part of the *demos*, democratic theorists since Plato have taught us that the people, while being sovereign, require structures that limit their participation.
>
> (1999: 132)

Not only is participation limited, it is typically limited in ways that confirm existing power imbalances: 'under conditions of structural inequality, normal processes of deliberation often in practice restrict access to agents with greater resources, knowledge, or connections to those with greater control over the forum' (Young, 2001: 680). Even at the very local level, Young sums up a number of barriers to participation by 'anyone with an interest':

> Even when a series of public hearings are announced for an issue, people who might wish to speak at them need to know about them, be able to arrange their work and child care schedule to be able to attend, be able to get to them, and have enough understanding of the hearing process to participate. Each of these abilities is unevenly present among members of a society.
>
> (ibid.: 680)

These constraints are of course multiplied at the global level. Discussions of these inequalities often focus rather crudely on geographical representation. What is interesting about the ICC negotiations is that in terms of this issue of 'Southern participation', global civil society performed rather well. There were substantial numbers of African and Latin American groups, although fewer Asian ones and very few from the Middle East (see Chapter 2). As discussed in Chapter 2, various 'causes' or 'issue areas', sometimes at odds with each other, were represented, although human rights concerns dominated.

However, in other ways the group of global civil society participants was very homogeneous. Almost without exception, they belonged to an English-speaking, university-educated, computer-literate middle class. Perhaps this is inevitable. To a lesser extent, this is also true of national parliamentarians. But it does not reflect the diversity of the world population, nor does it necessarily reflect the profile of future victims of war crimes, crimes against humanity or genocide.

In fact, there appear to have been surprisingly few victims of past human rights violations involved in the negotiations. Barnes de Carlotto, the Abuela described above, was one of them, as was Raquel Edralin-Tigalo, an anti-torture activist from the Philippines who had herself been subject to torture (Bliss, 1998). Another participant with personal knowledge of one of the issues at stake was Robert Green, a former naval commander who had flown anti-submarine helicopters which carried nuclear weapons, and who had later become an anti-nuclear activist (Jackson, 1998c). Others had worked closely with victims, but most of the legal experts present at the negotiations had primarily theoretical knowledge of the crimes at stake. It is of course not necessary to have suffered human rights violations, or to have insider knowledge of nuclear devastation, to have a viewpoint about the ICC, based for instance on legal expertise or on moral conviction. But if participation in global processes is necessarily selective on practical grounds, then a particular effort should be made, particularly within global civil society, but also by global institutions, to include the voices of 'experiential experts': on human rights violations, on HIV/AIDS, or on child soldiers, and not just technical ones. In other fora, such as trade negotiations, non-governmental organisations and networks have engaged in 'accompaniment', for instance of small farmers who would be affected by the negotiations (Edelman, 2003: 210–211). Such practices could aid inclusion of 'experiential experts', provided they offer real participation, and not a symbolic trotting out of 'the victim' to support the NGO's already formed position.

Thus, the idea of 'participation' as an alternative to representation is limited by exclusion. There are those who exclude themselves and those who are deliberately excluded by states, but the most intractable form of exclusion is that by class, means, education and information. Global institutions and global civil society should be able to do more to include the voices of poorer, less educated people with a clear stake in the negotiations than it did in the ICC case, but in the world as it is, it is very doubtful that such inclusion can ever be much more than symbolic.

Conclusion

A deficit remains

On the basis of the ICC case, it can be argued that global civil society greatly contributed to strengthening certain features commonly associated with democratic procedure, in particular transparency, equality and deliberation. Global civil society should not be seen as offering a form of representation of the global *demos*, however, or at least not representation in its traditional form. It could be conceptualised as a form of participation, but in practice this participation is so limited and so uneven that global civil society cannot entirely be considered an adequate 'functional equivalent' or 'alternative mechanism' to parliamentary democracy, operating at the global level.

Global civil society in its present form cannot be considered a satisfactory substitute for democracy, and there is no reason to believe it will make great strides in that direction. It does contribute to making international decision-making processes more democratic than they were before, but a democratic deficit remains. However, it can be argued that another contribution is made by global civil society to international decision-making processes, one that has received much less attention than the democratising aspect: that of moral values.

Global ethics

The hundreds of groups and individuals who engaged in the ICC negotiations, whether they were criminal law experts, pro-family groups or world federalists, all became involved because of their belief in, or concerns about, a particular kind of Court. For some, such as the law students of ELSA, career considerations may have played something of a role. For some NGO professionals, it was 'their job' to be there. But their involvement went far beyond that of an ordinary job. Often, they had had to convince their own organisations of the importance of being there. The overriding motivation for being involved was based on ethical convictions.

But what of the state representatives; do they have ethical convictions? There are two classic theories in international relations on foreign policy and ethics. The first, and certainly the most influential until the 1990s, is realism. Based on a particular reading of Machiavelli, or alternatively a transposition of Hobbes' 'war of every man against every man' theory to the international plane (Walker, 1993), it teaches that international relations are an anarchical sphere where each state pursues its national interest and there is no place for ethics. Liberal or idealist theory, on the contrary, teaches that there is a 'society of states', where rules in the common interest of humankind are constructed and, for the most part, obeyed (see, for instance, Russett *et al.*, 2004: 25–27). According to the latter theory, there is a space for 'ethics', or enlightened self-interest, in foreign policy. It also gives more space to the conceptualisation of intergovernmental organisations, and sometimes even civil society groups, as independent actors. But neither theory really understands the diplomats themselves as social actors subject to environmental influences (the social constructivist school does; see, for instance, Onuf, 1989; Walker, 1993). Whether it is 'national interest' or a more cooperative stance, the policies of states are conceptualised as holy writ, handed down from black-box foreign ministries. State representatives are not to have convictions, ethical or otherwise.

In reality, state representatives do, of course, have value dispositions of their own. As discussed in Chapter 2, many of the diplomats of the influential Like-Minded Group were ardent supporters of the Court, not just professionally but also personally. Their prolific writing on the ICC (see, for instance, the contributions to Lee (1999b, 2001); Von Hebel *et al.* (1999); and the special issue of the *European Journal of Crime, Criminal Law and Criminal Justice* (1998), to mention just a few) attests to this, as does the fact that four have since been elected as judges to the Court, and others now work in the Prosecutor's Office (ICC website).

Nor are state positions on something like the ICC arrived at in isolation from those who negotiate on them. They are gradually formed, informed by inside expertise and outside information, and constantly readjusted. The atmosphere of the negotiations can influence the substance of the positions. As discussed in this chapter, global civil society transformed that atmosphere in terms of transparency and deliberation. But another aspect of the sustained presence of civil society actors was that they constantly invoked ethical considerations, claims about the needs of humankind. In Rome, their numbers swelled to approximately 450 people, collectively by far the largest delegation at the Rome conference (Pace, 1999: 202).

International relations theories such as realism and idealism do not just seek to explain state behaviour – or, as I would rather put it, the behaviour of state representatives – they also end up informing such behaviour. In domestic politics, it is not ethically acceptable for politicians to defend policies simply as being in the self-interest of a particular group: 'this policy is good for the small businessmen, or for the Catholic minority, who vote for me'. They need to present such policies as being for the common good: 'small businesses will kick-start the national economy', 'Catholic emancipation will make our society more equitable'. The dominance of realist theory made any such arguments for the general interest unnecessary in the international sphere – it even characterised them as foolish. It legitimised the invocation of a (flexibly definable) 'national interest' by diplomats as the sole motivation for this or that position.

Global civil society actors present themselves precisely as the champion of values beyond state interests, working towards a global common good. Having a majority of such actors around is like being accompanied to a brothel by a delegation of priests. Even without having any formal status, they constrain behaviour and change the terms of debate. Forthright statements that 'this is not in our nation's interest' can still be heard in international negotiations, but they jar in an environment where appeals to reason and to universal justice are increasingly common currency. States are therefore more motivated to frame their proposals in terms of appropriateness and justice in the presence of civil society actors. In some cases, state representatives themselves completely took over the moral high ground that usually belongs to civil society actors: the passionate appeals of Bosnian and Burundian delegates for various forms of gender justice, based on experiences in their own countries, in every way resembled activist advocacy.

If it is accepted that global civil society moves states towards appreciating, or at least appearing to appreciate, 'ethical' or 'common good' arguments over national interest arguments in international negotiations, the question remains which ethical projects make it to those fora, and get taken up. In the ICC negotiations, while there was some open (women's groups versus pro-family groups) as well as some muted contestation (around weapons of mass destruction), there was clearly a dominant civil society project: to prise away from the exclusive domain of states the power to punish perpetrators of genocide, war crimes and crimes against humanity. Those who do not like the project will point to the democratic deficit of global civil society: the lack of representation and limits to participation. They are likely to point back to national democracy as the solution.

The existence of a democratic deficit at the global level, and the fact that global civil society cannot entirely fill it, should not be denied. But the number of victims made by human rights violating states in the last century is staggering. Some of these governments were flawed democracies, too. This is why it is worth giving up some national democratic supremacy in exchange for international law, first to frame norms on human rights, disarmament and the environment, and second to actually enforce them. And global civil society should be there to help make these laws and get them enforced, to strengthen transparency, equality and deliberation in international decision-making processes, and to help inch states from narrow interests to global common interests. Those who think that this is not in fact in the interest of humanity should come and join the debate with their own ethical project – become part of global civil society.

References

ABA (American Bar Association) (1998). 'Recommendation on the International Criminal Court'. 2 February.

'ABCs of the ICC' (1996). *ICC Monitor 1*. July/August.

AI (Amnesty International) (1991). *Mexico: Torture with Impunity*. London: AI.

—— (1994). *Establishing a Just, Fair and Effective International Criminal Court*. London: AI.

—— (1997). *The International Criminal Court: Making the Right Choices, Part I: Defining the Crimes and Permissible Defences and Initiating a Prosecution*. January.

—— (1998a). *The International Criminal Court: Making the Right Choices, Part V: Recommendations to the Diplomatic Conference*. May.

—— (1998b). 'International Criminal Court. Final Statement at the Diplomatic Conference Delivered by Pierre Sané.' 16 July.

—— (1998c). 'International Criminal Court – "Crippled at Birth?" Press release. 17 July.

'Aims and Objectives of the International War Crimes Tribunal' (1968). In John Duffet (ed.), *Against the Crime of Silence: Proceedings of the Russell International War Crimes Tribunal*. New York, London: O'Hare Books, Bertrand Russell Peace Foundation.

Almeida, Iris (1999). 'Civil Society and the Establishment of the International Criminal Court'. In Maureen McCarthy and Patricia Brown (eds), *Civil Society Engaging Multilateral Institutions: At the Crossroads*. Montreal: Proceedings from the First Forum.

'An Appeal from Four Major Human Rights Organizations' (1998). *On the Record*, vol. 1, no. 19, Part 1. 13 July.

Anderson, Kenneth (2000). 'The Ottawa Convention Banning Landmines, the Role of International Non-governmental Organizations and the Idea of International Civil Society'. *European Journal of International Law*, vol. 11, no. 1, pp. 91–120.

Anheier, Helmut, Glasius, Marlies and Kaldor, Mary (2001). 'Introducing Global Civil Society'. In Helmut Anheier, Marlies Glasius and Mary Kaldor (eds), *Global Civil Society 2001*. Oxford: Oxford University Press.

Annan, Kofi (1998). 'The Gift of Hope to Future Generations'. Statement at the Adoption of the Statute of the International Criminal Court at the United Nations Diplomatic Conference, Rome, 18 July. Reproduced in *ICC Monitor* 9. August.

Arsanjani, Mahnoush (1999). 'Reflections on the Jurisdiction and Trigger Mechanism of the International Criminal Court', in Herman A. M. von Hebel, Johan G. Lammers and Jolien Schukking (eds), *Reflections on the International Criminal Court: Essays in Honour of Adriaan Bos*. The Hague: T. M. C. Asser Press.

Artucio, Alejandro (1992a). *A Breach of Impunity. The Trial for the Murder of Jesuits in El Salvador: Report of the Trial Observer of the International Commission of Jurists*. New York: Fordham University Press.

—— (1992b). 'Impunity of Perpetrators'. In Theo van Boven, Cees Flinterman, Fred Grunfeld and Ingrid Westendorp (eds) *Seminar on the Right to Restitution, Compensation and Rehabilitation for Victims of Gross Violations of Human Rights and Fundamental Freedoms*. SIM Special no. 12. Utrecht.

Austin, Karen (1998). 'Small Victories: Children's Rights under the International Criminal Court'. *Human Rights Tribune*, vol. 5, no. 4. September.

Barber, Benjamin (1984). *Strong Democracy: Participatory Politics for a New Age*. Berkeley: University of California Press.

Bassiouni, M. Cherif (1996). 'An Idea Whose Time Has Come'. *Chicago Tribune*. 18 June.

—— (comp., 1999). *The Statute of the International Criminal Court: A Documentary History*. Dordrecht: Martinus Nijhoff.

Bedont, Barbara and Hall Martinez, Katherine (1999). 'Ending Impunity for Gender Crimes under the International Criminal Court'. *Brown Journal of World Affairs*, vol. 6, no. 1, pp. 65–85.

Beetham, David (1999). *Democracy and Human Rights*. Cambridge: Polity Press.

Beigbeder, Yves (1999). *Judging War Criminals: The Politics of International Justice*. Basingstoke, UK: Macmillan.

Benedetti, Fanny (1997). 'A Report on the Negotiations for the Creation of an International Criminal Court'. *Human Rights Brief*, vol. 5, no. 1. Fall.

Benedetti, Fanny and Washburn, John (1999). 'Drafting the International Criminal Court Treaty: Two Years to Rome and an Afterword on the Rome Diplomatic Conference'. *Global Governance*, vol. 5, pp. 1–37.

Bergsmo, Morten (1998). 'The Jurisdictional Regime of the International Criminal Court (Part II, Articles 11–19)'. *European Journal of Crime, Criminal Law and Criminal Justice*, no. 4, pp. 345–363.

Bessette, Joseph (1980). 'Deliberative Democracy: The Majority Principle in Republican Government'. In Robert A. Goldwin and William A. Schambra (eds) *How Democratic Is the Constitution?* Washington, DC: American Enterprise Institute for Public Policy Research.

Blaug, Ricardo (1999). Democracy, Real and Ideal: Discourse Ethics and Radical Politics. Albany: State University of New York Press.

Bliss, Anna (1998). 'Over 70% of Victims of War are Women and Children, Say Campaigners'. *On the Record*, vol. 1, no. 10, Part 2. 30 June.

Boissier, Pierre (1963). *Histoire du Comité International de la Croix-Rouge: De Solferino à Tsoushima*. Paris: Plon.

Boon, Kristen (2001). 'Rape and Forced Pregnancy under the ICC Statute: Human Dignity, Autonomy and Consent'. *Columbia Human Rights Law Review*, vol. 32, no. 3, pp. 625–675.

Bos, Adriaan (1999). 'The International Criminal Court: Recent Developments'. In Herman A. M. von Hebel, Johan G. Lammers and Jolien Schukking (eds), *Reflections on the International Criminal Court: Essays in Honour of Adriaan Bos*. The Hague: T. M. C. Asser Press.

Bradley, Curtis (2002). 'U.S. Announces Intent Not to Ratify International Criminal Court Treaty'. *American Society of International Law Insights*. May.

'British Allies, NGOs Furious at Broad UK Campaign to "neutralise" ICC' (1998). *On the Record*, vol. 1, no. 10 (Part 2). 30 June.

Broomhall, Bruce (1998). 'An Overview of NGO Positions on Key ICC Issues'. *ICC Monitor 8*. June.

Bunch, Charlotte with Peggy Anthrobus, Samantha Frost and Niamh Reilly (2001). 'International Networking for Women's Human Rights'. In M. Edwards and J. Gaventa (eds), *Global Citizen Action*. London: Earthscan.

Bureau Discussion Paper on Part 2 (Jurisdiction, Admissibility and Applicable Law) (1998). UN Doc. A/CONF.183/C.1/L.53. 7 July.

Bureau Proposal on Part 2 (Jurisdiction, Admissibility and Applicable Law) (1998). UN Doc. A/CONF.183/C.1/L.59. 10 July.

Burgers, Jan Herman (1992). 'The Road to San Francisco: The Revival of the Human Rights Idea in the Twentieth Century'. *Human Rights Quarterly*, vol. 14, no. 4, pp. 447–477.

Burroughs, John (1999). 'The International Criminal Court, Weapons of Mass Destruction, NGOs, and Other Issues': A Report on the Negotiations and the Statute'. April. http://www.lcnp.org/global/icc.htm.

Burroughs, John and Cabasso, Jacqueline (1999). 'Confronting the Nuclear-Armed States in International Negotiating Forums: Lessons for NGOs'. *International Negotiation*, vol. 4, pp. 457–480.

Busdachin, Marino (1997). 'ICC Appeal Gathers Hundreds of Signatures'. *ICC Monitor 3*, p. 8. January.

'Canada Slammed by Peace Activists for "Timidity" on Landmines' (1998). *On the Record*, vol. 1, no. 4. 18 June.

Carter, April (1992). *International Protest and World Politics since 1945*. London: Longman.

Cassese, Antonio (1996a) 'Introduction'. In International Tribunal for the Prosecution of Persons Responsible for Serious Violations of International Humanitarian Law Committed in the Territory of the Former Yugoslavia since 1991. *The Path to The Hague: Selected Documents on the Origins of the ICTY*.

—— (1996b). *Memorandum to Members of the Preparatory Committee on the Establishment of an International Criminal Court*. 22 March.

C-FAM (Catholic Family and Human Rights Institute). (1997a). 'Rome Makes Urgent Call for Life and Family Voices at UN Conferences'. *Friday Fax*, vol. 1, no. 9. 21 November.

—— (1997b). 'International Criminal Court Takes a Giant Step in UN General Assembly'. *Friday Fax*, vol. 1, no. 12. 19 December.

—— (1998a). 'Last Minute Holy See Proposal May Guarantee Debate on "Enforced Pregnancy" at International Criminal Court in Rome'. *Friday Fax*. Special Edition 2. 6 April.

—— (1998b). 'Feminists Refuse to Define Their "Gender Agenda" for the International Criminal Court'. *Friday Fax*, vol. 1, no. 37. 26 June.

—— (1998c). 'Catholic, Muslim Nations Unite against "Enforced Pregnancy" and "Gender Justice"'. *Friday Fax*, vol. 1, no. 39. 10 July.

—— (1998d). 'Rome Conference Ends without Consensus for Creating International Criminal Court', *Friday Fax*, vol. 1, no. 40. 18 July.

'Chairman Struggles to Define Compromise Package' (1998). *On the Record*, vol. 1, no. 14. 7 July.

Charnovitz, Steve (1997). 'Two Centuries of Participation: NGOs and International Governance'. *Michigan Journal of International Law*, vol. 18, no. 2, pp. 171–190.

'China and France Shut the Door on Victims' Parents' (1998). *On the Record*, vol. 1, no. 3. 17 June.

'China Scuttles NGO Meet on Child Victims' (1998). *Terra Viva*. 17 June.

CICC (Coalition for an International Criminal Court) (1998a). 'Basic Principles for an Independent, Effective and Fair International Criminal Court'. May.

—— (1998b). 'The Numbers: NGO Coalition Special Report on Country Positions'. *The Rome Treaty Conference CICC Monitor*. Special Report. 10 July.

—— (1998c). 'The Virtual Vote, NGO Coalition Special Report on Country Positions on L. 59'. 13 July.

—— (2004a). 'Summary of Information on Bilateral Immunity Agreements (BIAs) or So-Called "Article 98" Agreements as of May 27, 2004'. 27 May.

—— (2004b). 'Status of Us Bilateral Immunity Agreements (BIAs)'. 15 July.

'CICC Team Reports' (1998). *On the Record*, vol. 1, no. 20. 14 July.

Clark, Ann Marie (2001). *Diplomacy of Conscience: Amnesty International and Changing Human Rights Norms*. Princeton, NJ: Princeton University Press.

Clark, Roger (2002). 'The Rome Statute of the International Criminal Court and Weapons of a Nature to Cause Superfluous Injury or Unnecessary Suffering, or Which Are Inherently Indiscriminate'. In John Carey, William Dunlap and R. John Pritchard (eds), *International Humanitarian Law: Challenges*. Ardsley, NY: Transnational Publishers.

Clark, Roger S. and Slade, Tuiloma Neroni (1999). 'Preamble and Final Clauses'. In Roy S. Lee (ed.), *The International Criminal Court: The Making of the Rome Statute: Issues, Negotiations, Results*. The Hague: Kluwer Law International.

Clinton, Bill (2000). 'Statement on Signature of the International Criminal Court Treaty'. Washington, DC. 31 December.

Cohen, Joshua and Joel Rogers (1983). *On Democracy: Toward a Transformation of American Society*. Harmondsworth UK: Penguin.

Cohen, Robin and Rai, Shirin (eds) (2000). *Global Social Movements*. London: Athlone.

'The Compromise Package: Analysis' (1998). *On the Record*, vol. 1, no. 15, part 1. 8 July.

Conso, Giovanni (1999). 'Looking to the Future'. In Roy S. Lee (ed.), *The International Criminal Court: The Making of the Rome Statute: Issues, Negotiations, Results*. The Hague: Kluwer Law International.

'A Court Is Born' (1998). *On the Record*, vol. 1, no. 22. 17 July.

Crawford, Teresa (1998). 'Strong Lobbying Efforts of Latin American NGO's Impacted the Rome Conference'. *On the Record,* vol. 1, no. 23, part 2. 27 July.

Déclaration Interprétative de la France [Interpretative Declaration of France] (2000). 9 June.

Deen, Thalif (2004). 'Facing Humiliating Defeat, US Abandons Move to Exempt Troops from War Crimes', *Inter Press Service*. 23 June.

Dickens, Alison (1998). 'As Second Week Begins, Outline of Workable Court Looms'. *Terra Viva*. 23 June.

Durham, Helen (2000a). 'Women and Civil Society: NGOs and International Criminal Law'. In K. Askin and D. Koenig (eds), *Women and International Human Rights Law,* vol. 3. Ardsley, NY: Transnational Publishers.

—— (2000b). 'The Role of NGOs in Creating the International Criminal Court Statute' (unpublished Ph.D. thesis). Melbourne: University of Melbourne.

'Dutch Disbelief at American Defeatism' (1998). *On the Record,* vol. 1, no. 4. 18 June.

Edelman, Marc (2003). 'Transnational Peasant and Farmer Movements'. In M. Kaldor, H. Anheier and M. Glasius (eds), *Global Civil Society 2003*. Oxford: Oxford University Press.

Edwards, Michael (2003) 'NGO Legitimacy: Voice or Vote?'. *BOND Networker*. February.

Edwards, Michael and John Gaventa (eds) (2001). *Global Citizen Action*. London: Earthscan.

ELSA (European Law Students Association) (1996). 'Trigger Mechanisms (the Role of the Prosecutor)' (Working Paper). Brussels: ELSA.

EN (Equality Now) (1995). 'Recommendations for the Draft Statute for an International Criminal Court'. New York: EN. April.

EP (European Parliament) (1998). Resolution on the International Criminal Court, adopted unanimously, 12 March.

Erb, Nicole Eva (1998). 'Gender-based Crimes under the Draft Statute for the Permanent International Criminal Court'. *Columbia Human Rights Law Review*, vol. 29, pp. 401–435.

European Journal of Crime, Criminal Law and Criminal Justice (1998). Special Issue on the International Criminal Court. vol. 6, no. 4. December.

'European Parliament: No Compromise on Principles' (1998). *Terra Viva*. 19 June.

Evans, James. (1998). 'Pro-lifers Win Limits on New UN Criminal Court'. *The Interim*. August.

Facio, Alda (1997). 'A Word (or Two) about Gender'. *ICC Monitor* 6. November.

—— (1998, unpublished). 'The Rome Diplomatic Conference: A Report'. In the author's possession.

Faith-Based Caucus (1997). 'Foundation Statement'. http://www.iccnow.org/html/faith.html

—— (1998). 'Draft Preamble, The Statute of the International Criminal Court'. http://www.iccnow.org/romearchive/papers/6PrepCmt/FaithBasedRecomm.pdf

Feakes, Daniel (2003). 'Global Civil Society and Biological and Chemical Weapons'. In Mary Kaldor, Helmut Anheier and Marlies Glasius (eds), *Global Civil Society 2003*. Oxford: Oxford University Press.

Ferencz, Benjamin (1980). *An International Criminal Court: A Step towards World Peace – A Documentary History and Analysis*. vol. 1: *Half a Century of Hope*. London: Oceana.

Fernández de Gurmendi, Silvia A. (1999). 'The Process of Negotiations'. In Roy S. Lee (ed.), *The International Criminal Court: The Making of the Rome Statute: Issues, Negotiations, Results*. The Hague: Kluwer Law International.

FIDH (Fédération Internationale des Ligues des Droits de l'Homme). 1997. Position Paper. August.

Florini, Ann M. (ed.) (2000) *The Third Force: The Rise of Transnational Civil Society*. Tokyo and Washington: Japan Center for International Exchange and Carnegie Endowment for Peace.

'French Position on War Crimes Sours French Support for Prosecutor, Reparations' (1998). *On the Record*, vol. 1, no. 18. 11 July.

Friedman, Elisabeth (1995). 'Women's Human Rights: The Emergence of a Movement'. In J. Peters and A. Wolper (eds), *Women's Rights Human Rights: International Feminist Pespectives*. New York: Routledge.

'Fury at Proposal to Omit Aggression and Use of Nuclear Weapons from ICC Scope' (1998). *On the Record*, vol. 1, no. 20. 14 July.

GAERC (General Affairs & External Relations Council) (2002). 'International Criminal Court (ICC) – Council Conclusions'. 30 September.

Goldman, Robert (1989). *Challenging Impunity: The Ley de Caducidad and the Referendum Campaign in Uruguay*. New York: Americas Watch.

Gonzalez Cueva, Eduardo (1998). 'Latin American and Caribbean Parliamentarians Issue Declaration in Support of ICC'. *ICC Monitor 8*, p. 11. June.

'Governments and Civil Society Meet in Dakar on the Court' (1998). *ICC Monitor* 7, p. 13. April.

Groulx, Elise (1997). 'Call for an International Criminal Defence Attorneys' Association'. *ICC Monitor 4*. May.

Guest, Ian. (1998). 'A Positive Mood, a Good Start, but a Lot of Questions'. *On the Record*, vol. 1, no. 7. 23 June.

Gutmann, Amy and Thompson, Dennis (1996). *Democracy and Disagreement*. Cambridge, MA: Belknap Press.

Hall, Christopher Keith (1997a). 'The First and Second Sessions of the UN Preparatory Committee on the Establishment of an International Criminal Court'. *American Journal of International Law*, vol. 91, pp. 177–187.

—— (1997b). 'Origins of the ICC Concept (1872-1945)'. *ICC Monitor* 6. November.

—— (1998a). 'The Third and Fourth Sessions of the UN Preparatory Committee on the Establishment of an International Criminal Court'. *American Journal of International Law*, vol. 92, pp. 124–133.

—— (1998b). 'The Fifth Session of the UN Preparatory Committee on the Establishment of an International Criminal Court'. *American Journal of International Law*, vol. 92, pp. 331–339.

Haq, Farhan (1998a). 'Compromise Shaping Up? US Mutes Stance on Council's Power'. *Terra Viva*. 18 June.

—— (1998b). 'Alliances Cut through North–South Divide'. *Terra Viva*. 22 June.

—— (1998c). 'Momentum Builds behind Powerful Prosecutor'. *Terra Viva*. 23 June.

—— (1998d). 'Non-Aligned Nations Target Nukes'. *Terra Viva*. 26 June.

—— (1998e). 'Canada Floats Compromise'. *Terra Viva*. 7 July.

—— (1998f). 'Speak Now (or Forever Hold Your Peace)'. *Terra Viva*. 8 July.

—— (1998g). 'What a Letdown!'. *Terra Viva*. 10 July.

Held, David (1995). *Democracy and the Global Order: From the Modern State to Cosmopolitan Governance*. Cambridge: Polity Press.

—— (2002). 'Globalization after September 11th. Global Transformations website, Polity Press. http://www.polity.co.uk/global/after_sept11.htm.

Howell, Jude and Pearce, Jenny (2001). *Civil Society and Development: A Critical Exploration*. Boulder, CO: Lynne Rienner.

HRW (Human Rights Watch) (1996). *Commentary for the Preparatory Committee on the Establishment of an International Criminal Court*. New York: HRW. August.

—— (1998a). *Justice in the Balance: Recommendations for an Independent and Effective International Criminal Court*. June 1998.

—— (1998b). '"Fight to the Finish" on International Criminal Court. Press release. Rome. 17 July.

—— (1998c). 'Human Rights Watch Textual Analysis International Criminal Court Treaty'. Press release. Rome. 17 July, 10 p.m.

—— (2002). 'U.S.: "Hague Invasion Act" Becomes Law. White House

"Stops at Nothing" in Campaign against War Crimes Court'. New York. 3 August.

'Human Rights Watch Appeal for Action and Key Issues Impacting the Court' (1998). *On the Record*, vol. 1, no. 19, part 1. 13 July.

IANSA (International Action Network on Small Arms) (1998). 'Founding Document of IANSA'. http://www.iansa.org/about/m1.htm.

'ICC: Promise of Justice or Threat of Tyranny?' (1998). *The Interim*. August.

ICJ (International Commission of Jurists) (1995). *The International Criminal Court* (Third ICJ Position Paper). Geneva: ICJ. August.

ICRC (International Committee of the Red Cross) (1997a). War Crimes: Working Paper prepared by the ICRC for the United Nations Preparatory Committee for the Establishment of an International Criminal Court, New York. 14 February.

—— (1997b). 'State Consent vs. Universal Jurisdiction'. 10 December.

—— (1998a). United Nations Diplomatic Conference of Plenipotentiaries on the Establishment of an International Criminal Court: Statement by Mr Cornelio Sommaruga, President of the International Committee of the Red Cross'. 16 June.

—— (1998b). 'Statement on the Establishment of an International Criminal Court'. 18 July.

ILC (International Law Commission) (1993). *Yearbook of the International Law Commission 1990*. Vol. 1: *Summary Records of the Forty-second session*. New York: United Nations.

—— (1997). 'Draft Statute for an International Criminal Court'. *Yearbook of the International Law Commission 1994*. Vol. 2, part 2: *Report of the Commission to the General Assembly on the Work of Its Forty-sixth session*. New York: United Nations.

'India, a Headache for its Allies' (1998). *Terra Viva*. 16 July.

'India and US Broadsides Threaten Consensus, Raise Prospect of Votes on Nuclear Weapons and Jurisdiction' (1998). *On the Record*, vol. 1, no. 21. 16 July.

'Indict Zedillo First, Protesters Demand' (1998). *Terra Viva*. 6 July.

International Law Association (1927). *Report of the Thirty-fourth Conference Held at the Imperial Palace and at the Chamber of Commerce, Vienna, August 5th to August 11th, 1926*. London: Sweet & Maxwell. Reproduced in Ferencz, Benjamin (1980). *An International Criminal Court: A Step towards World Peace – A Documentary History and Analysis*. Vol. 1: *Half a Century of Hope*. London: Oceana.

Interpretative Declaration made by the Government of New Zealand on Ratification of the Rome Statute of the International Criminal Court (2000).

IPB (International Peace Bureau) (1997). 'International Criminal Court: Analysis of Issues and Recommendations for Action'. Briefing Paper. July.

Jackson, Rochelle (1998a). 'On the Trail of the Dictators, in Search of a Missing Child: Estela Barnes de Carlotto, President of the Abuelas de Plaza de Mayo'. *On the Record*, vol. 1, no. 2. 16 June.

—— (1998b). 'Profile: Richard Goldstone: Golden Advice from a Former Prosecutor'. *On the Record,* vol. 1, no. 7. 23 June.

—— (1998c). 'From Nuclear Whizz-Kid to Pacifist: Commander Robert Green'. *On the Record,* vol. 1, no. 12. 3 July.

Jaura, Ramesh (1998). 'India Thumbs Nose at "European" Court'. *Terra Viva.* 17 July.

Joachim, Jutta (1999). 'Shaping the Human Rights Agenda: The Case of Violence against Women'. In M. Meyer and E. Pruegl (eds), *Gender Politics in Global Governance.* Lanham, MD: Rowman & Littlefield.

Kaldor, Mary (2001) 'A Decade of Humanitarian Intervention: The Role of Global Civil Society'. In Helmut Anheier, Marlies Glasius and Mary Kaldor (eds), *Global Civil Society 2001.* Oxford: Oxford University Press.

—— (2003). *Global Civil Society: An Answer to War.* Cambridge: Polity Press.

Kant, Immanuel (1991). 'Perpetual Peace: A Philosophical Sketch' (first published 1795). In Kant, Immanuel, *Political Writings*, edited by Hans Reiss. Cambridge: Cambridge University Press.

Kaul, Hans-Peter (1998). 'Special Note: The Struggle for the International Criminal Court's Jurisdiction'. *European Journal of Crime, Criminal Law and Criminal Justice*, vol. 6, no. 4, pp. 364–376.

Keck, Margaret and Sikkink, Kathryn (1998). 'Transnational Networks on Violence against Women'. In M. Keck and K. Sikkink, *Activists beyond Borders: Advocacy Networks in International Politics*. Ithaca, NY: Cornell University Press.

Kirk, Alejandro (1998a). 'Desaparecidos, A Festering Wound'. *Terra Viva.* 24 June.

—— (1998b). 'Treaty? What Treaty?'. *Terra Viva.* 13 July.

—— (1998c). 'High Noon'. *Terra Viva.* 15 July.

Kirsch, Philippe (1999). 'The Development of the Rome Statute'. In Roy S. Lee (ed.), *The International Criminal Court: The Making of the Rome Statute: Issues, Negotiations, Results.* The Hague: Kluwer Law International.

Kirsch, Philippe and Holmes, John T. (1999). 'The Birth of the International Criminal Court: The 1998 Rome Conference'. In *The Canadian Yearbook of International Law*, vol. 36. Vancouver: UBC Press.

Klarin, Mirko (1991). 'Nuremberg Now!'. *Borba*, 16 May. Reproduced (translated) in International Tribunal for the Prosecution of Persons Responsible for Serious Violations of International Humanitarian Law Committed in the Territory of the Former Yugoslavia since 1991, *The Path to The Hague: Selected Documents on the Origins of the ICTY.* 1996.

Klinghofer, Arthur Jay and Klinghofer, Judith Apter (2002). *International Citizens' Tribunals: Mobilizing Public Opinion to Advance Human Rights.* New York: Palgrave.

Krieger, David (1998). 'The Nuremberg Promise and the International Criminal Court'. Nuclear Age Peace Foundation. December. http://www.wagingpeace .org/articles/nuremberg.html.

Kulczycki, Andrzej (1999). *The Abortion Debate in the World Arena*. Basingstoke, UK: Macmillan.

LCHR (Lawyers Committee for Human Rights) (1991). *Impunity: Prosecutions of Human Rights Violations in the Philippines*. New York: Lawyers Committee for Human Rights.

—— (1996). 'Establishing an International Criminal Court: Major Unresolved Issues in the Draft Statute Position Paper'. August.

—— (1998a). 'Establishing an International Criminal Court: Major Unresolved Issues in the Draft Statute – Revised and Updated'. *International Criminal Court Briefing Series*, vol. 1, no. 1. May.

—— (1998b). Exercise of ICC Jurisdiction: The Case for Universal Jurisdiction. Lawyers Committee for Human Rights *International Criminal Court Briefing Series*, vol. 1, no. 8. May.

—— (1998c). 'Response to US Concerns regarding the Proposal for a Proprio Motu Prosecutor'. New York: LCHR. 24 June.

—— (1998d). 'Lawyers Committee for Human Rights Denounces Jurisdiction Provisions of ICC Proposal'. Press release. 17 July.

—— (1998e). 'International Criminal Court Treaty Adopted at Rome Conference'. Press release. 17 July.

LCNP (Lawyers' Committee on Nuclear Policy (2000). 'The French "Interpretative Declaration" Regarding Nuclear Weapons'. 5 July.

Lee, Roy S. (1999a). 'Introduction: The Rome Conference and Its Contributions to International Law'. In Roy S. Lee (ed.), *The International Criminal Court: The Making of the Rome Statute: Issues, Negotiations, Results*. The Hague: Kluwer Law International.

—— (ed.) (1999b). *The International Criminal Court: The Making of the Rome Statute; Issues, Negotiations, Results*. The Hague: Kluwer Law International.

—— (ed.) (2001). *The International Criminal Court: Elements of Crimes and Rules of Procedure and Evidence*. Ardsley, NY: Transnational Publishers.

Lewis, David (2002). 'Civil Society in African Contexts: Reflections on the Usefulness of a Concept'. *Development and Change*, vol. 33, no. 4, pp. 569–586.

'Lifesite Report on the Approval of the International Criminal Court' (1998). *LifeSite Daily News*. 19 July.

Lifton, Denise and Norris, Pascale (1997). 'Regional Reports'. *ICC Monitor* 6. November.

Lutz, Ellen (1990). *Human Rights in Mexico: A Policy of Impunity*. New York: Human Rights Watch.

McGrew, Anthony (1997). *The Transformation of Democracy? Globalization and Territorial Democracy*. Cambridge: Polity Press.

'Madres Thrown Out' (1998). *Terra Viva*. 18 June.

Meron, Theodor (1999). 'Crimes under the Jurisdiction of the International Criminal Court'. In Herman A. M. von Hebel, Johan G. Lammers and Jolien Schukking (eds), *Reflections on the International Criminal Court: Essays in Honour of Adriaan Bos*. The Hague: T. M. C. Asser Press.

'Movement on Admissibility Comes Slowly' (1998). *Terra Viva*. 2 July.

Nanda, Ved (1996). 'World Needs a Court for World Crimes'. *Denver Post*. 18 August.

'National Abortion Laws Will Not Be Undermined by Inclusion of Forced Pregnancy as a Crime against Humanity, Pledges Women's Caucus' (1998). *On the Record*, vol. 1, no. 9. 29 June.

Nel, Philip (2002). 'Between Counter-hegemony and Post-hegemony: The Rome Statute and Normative Innovation in World Politics'. In Andrew Cooper, John English and Ramesh Thakur (eds), *Enhancing Global Governance: Towards a New Diplomacy?* Tokyo: United Nations University Press.

'News Chronology November 1996 through February 1997' (1997). *Chemical Weapons Convention Bulletin*. March 1997.

'News Chronology November 1997 through February 1998' (1998a). *CBW Conventions Bulletin*. March 1998.

'News Chronology May 1998 through August 1998' (1998b). *CBW Conventions Bulletin*. September 1998.

'News Chronology November 1999 through January 2000' (2000). *CBW Conventions Bulletin*. March 2000.

'NGO Activities in Rome' (1998). *ICC Monitor 10*, p. 11. November.

Nsereko, Daniel (1997). 'Dr. Daniel Nsereko on the August PrepCom and Beyond'. *ICC Monitor* 6. November.

'Nuclear Cloud over War Crimes Debate' (1998). *On the Record*, vol. 1, no. 12. 3 July.

Onuf, Nicholas Greenwood (1989). *World of Our Making: Rules and Rule in Social Theory and International Relations*. Columbia: University of South Carolina Press.

Oosterveld, Valerie L. (1999). 'The Making of a Gender-Sensitive International Criminal Court'. *International Law FORUM du droit international*, vol. 1, no. 1, pp. 38–41. February.

'Opting In on War Crimes Would Be "Retrograde Step for International Law" Warns Angry Red Cross' (1998). *On the Record*, vol. 1, no. 20. 14 July.

Pace, William R. (1999). 'The Relationship between the International Criminal Court and Non-governmental Organizations'. In Herman A. M. von Hebel, Johan G. Lammers and Jolien Schukking (eds), *Reflections on the International Criminal Court: Essays in Honour of Adriaan Bos*. The Hague: T. M. C. Asser Press.

Pace, William R. and Thieroff, Mark (1999). 'Participation of Non-governmental Organizations', in Roy S. Lee (ed.), *The International Criminal Court: The Making of the Rome Statute; Issues, Negotiations, Results*. The Hague: Kluwer Law International.

Pace, William R. and Schense, Jennifer (2001). 'Coalition for the International Criminal Court at the Preparatory Commission', in Roy S. Lee (ed.), *The International Criminal Court: Elements of Crime and Rules of Procedure and Evidence*. New York: Transnational Publications.

Panganiban, Rik (1998). 'Show the Governments in Rome that the World is Watching'. *On the Record*, vol. 1, no. 16, part 2. 9 July.

Pateman, Carole (1970). *Participation and Democratic Theory*. London: Cambridge University Press.

Pax Romana (1996). 'Commentaries to the Draft Statute of the International Permanent Criminal Court (IPCC)'. Barcelona: Pax Romana. 28 March.

Peace Caucus (1998). 'Weapons Systems and the International Criminal Court'. Position Paper from the Peace Caucus for the International Criminal Court regarding the options in Article 5, War Crimes Section B (o).

Plakkaat van Verlatinghe [Act of Abjuration] (1581). 26 July. Available at http://www.burgerschapskunde.nl/onafhankelijkheid.html.

Popper, Karl R. (1952). *The Open Society and Its Enemies*. 2nd ed. (revised). London: Routledge & Kegan Paul, 2 vols.

PrepCom (Preparatory Committee on the Establishment of an International Criminal Court) (1997). 'Working Group on Definitions and Elements of Crimes: War Crimes'; Article 20 C. UN Doc. A/AC.249/1997/WG.1/CRP.9. 12 December.

'President of Uganda Refers Situation concerning the Lord's Resistance Army (LRA) to the ICC' (2004). Press release, International Criminal Court, The Hague. 29 January.

'Prosecutor Receives Referral of the Situation in the Democratic Republic of Congo' (2004). Press release, International Criminal Court, The Hague. 19 April.

REAL Women of Canada (1998a) 'The International Criminal Court – World Nightmare'. *REALity Newsletter*, vol. 16, no. 9.

—— (1998b) 'Canada Courts Disaster with World Court'. *REALity Newsletter*, vol. 16, no. 10.

'"Rebellious" Rome Conference Demands Curbs on Security Council Veto Power' (1998). *On the Record*, vol. 1, no. 7. 23 June.

'Regional Reports' (1997). *ICC Monitor* 6. November.

Robinson, Arthur N. R. (1999). Opening Address at the Inter-governmental Caribbean Conference on the International Criminal Court, Port of Spain. 19 March. http://www.theofficeofthepresident.gov.tt/InternationalCriminalCourt.htm.

Robinson, Mary (2000). Speaking on the occasion of International Women's Day. 8 March. Quoted at http://www.iccwomen.org/archive/index.html.

Roht-Arriaza, Naomi (ed.) (1995). *Impunity and Human Rights in International Law and Practice*. New York: Oxford University Press.

'Rome Conference Ends without Consensus' (1998). *Life Advocate Magazine*, vol. 13, no. 2. September/October.

Rome Statute of the International Criminal Court (1998). UN Doc. A/CONF. 183/9.

Rosenau, James (1998). 'Governance and Democracy in a Globalizing World'. In Daniele Archibugi, David Held and Martin Köhler (eds), *Re-imagining Political Community: Studies in Cosmopolitan Democracy*. Stanford, CA: Stanford University Press.

Russell, Bertrand (1968a). 'Message from Bertrand Russell to the Tribunal'. In John Duffet (ed.), *Against the Crime of Silence: Proceedings of the Russell International War Crimes Tribunal.* New York, London: O'Hare Books, Bertrand Russell Peace Foundation.

—— (1968b). 'Closing Address to the Stockholm Session'. In John Duffet (ed.), *Against the Crime of Silence: Proceedings of the Russell International War Crimes Tribunal.* New York, London: O'Hare Books, Bertrand Russell Peace Foundation.

Russett, Bruce, Harvey Starr and David Kinsella (2004). *World Politics: The Menu for Choice.* 7th ed. Melbourne: Thomson Wadsworth.

Said, Yahia and Desai, Meghnad (2003). 'Trade and Global Civil Society: The Anti-capitalist Movement Revisited'. In Mary Kaldor, Helmut Anheier and Marlies Glasius (eds), *Global Civil Society 2003.* Oxford: Oxford University Press.

Saland, Per (1999). 'International Criminal Law Principles'. In Roy S. Lee (ed.), *The International Criminal Court: The Making of the Rome Statute: Issues, Negotiations, Results.* The Hague: Kluwer Law International.

Sartre, Jean-Paul (1968) 'Jean-Paul Sartre's Inaugural Statement to the Tribunal'. In John Duffet (ed.), *Against the Crime of Silence: Proceedings of the Russell International War Crimes Tribunal.* New York, London: O'Hare Books, Bertrand Russell Peace Foundation.

Schabas, William (2001). *An Introduction to the International Criminal Court.* Cambridge: Cambridge University Press.

Scharf, Michael (1997). *Balkan Justice: The Story behind the First International War Crimes Trial since Nuremberg.* Durham, NC: Carolina Academic Press.

Scheffer, David J. (1999) 'The United States and the International Criminal Court'. *American Journal of International Law*, vol. 93, no. 1, pp. 12–22.

Scholte, Jan Aart (2001). *Civil Society and Democracy in Global Governance.* CSGR Working Paper no. 65/01. Warwick University, UK: Centre for the Study of Globalisation and Regionalisation.

Schwarzenberger, Georg (1968). *International Law as Applied by Courts and Tribunals.* Vol. 2: *The Law of Armed Conflict.* London: Stevens.

'Selections from Statements on ICC by Region' (1997). *ICC Monitor Special Edition*, pp. 6–7. December.

Seligman, Adam (1992) *The Idea of Civil Society.* New York: Free Press.

Sen, Purna (2003) 'Successes and Challenges: Understanding the Global Movement to End Violence against Women'. In Mary Kaldor, Helmut Anheier and Marlies Glasius (eds), *Global Civil Society 2003.* Oxford: Oxford University Press.

Sharratt, Sara and Kaschak, Ellyn (1999). *Assault on the Soul: Women in the Former Yugoslavia.* New York: Haworth Press.

Shaw, Martin (2000). *Theory of the Global State: Global Reality as an Unfinished Revolution.* Cambridge: Cambridge University Press.

Shriver, Donald W. (1997). 'The International Criminal Court: Its Moral Urgency'. *ICC Monitor* 7. February.

Sieder, Rachel (ed.) (1995). *Impunity in Latin America*. London: Institute of Latin American Studies.

Smith, Jackie, Charles Chatfield and Ron Pagnucco (eds) (1997) *Transnational Social Movements and World Politics: Solidarity beyond the State*. Syracuse, NY: Syracuse University Press.

'Special Analysis of the ICC Statute' (1998). *On the Record*, vol. 1, no. 8. 26 June.

Specific Decisions by the London Conference (1992). 27 August. Reproduced in International Tribunal for the Prosecution of Persons Responsible for Serious Violations of International Humanitarian Law Committed in the Territory of the Former Yugoslavia since 1991 (1996). *The Path to The Hague: Selected Documents on the Origins of the ICTY*.

'State Consent Could Weaken the Geneva Convention Warns Red Cross Chief' (1998), *On the Record*, vol. 1, no. 3. 17 June.

Statement by Trinidad and Tobago, speaking on behalf of the Caribbean Community (CARICOM) member states that were also Members of the United Nations. In 'Views and Comments by Governments', in Roy S. Lee (ed.), *The International Criminal Court: The Making of the Rome Statute: Issues, Negotiations, Results*. The Hague: Kluwer Law International.

Steains, Cate (1999). 'Gender Issues'. In Roy S. Lee (ed.), *The International Criminal Court: The Making of the Rome Statute: Issues, Negotiations, Results*. The Hague: Kluwer Law International.

Stoelting, David (1997). 'New York Bar Association Endorses ICC'. *ICC Monitor 3*. January.

'Support Growing for an Independent Prosecutor'. (1998) *On the Record*, vol. 1, no. 7. 23 June.

UN (United Nations) (1989). Request for the Inclusion of a Supplementary Item in the Agenda of the Forty-fourth session, International Criminal Responsibility of Individuals and Entities Engaged in Illicit Trafficking in Narcotic Drugs and across National Frontiers and Other Transnational Criminal Activities: Establishment of an International Criminal Court with Jurisdiction over Such Crimes, Letter dated 21 August 1989 from the Permanent Representative of Trinidad and Tobago to the United Nations addressed to the Secretary-General, 21 August 1989. Doc. A/44/195.

—— (1990) Resolution Adopted by the General Assembly, International Criminal Responsibility of Individuals and Entities Engaged in Illicit Trafficking in Narcotic Drugs across National Frontiers and Other Transnational Criminal Activities: Establishment of an International Criminal Court with Jurisdiction over Such Crimes, 18 January 1990. Doc. A/RES/44/39.

—— (1994). Resolution Adopted by the General Assembly, Establishment of an International Criminal Court, 9 December 1994. Doc. A/RES/49/53.

—— (1995a). 'Power of Security Council to Refer Cases to Proposed International Criminal Court Debated in Ad Hoc Committee'. Committee on International Criminal Court, First Session, 4th Meeting (PM). 4 April. Press release L/2716.

—— (1995b). 'Security Council's Right to Refer Cases to Proposed International Criminal Tribunal Discussed In Ad Hoc Committee'. Committee on International Criminal Court, First Session, 5th Meeting (AM). 5 April. Press release L/2717.
—— (1995c). 'Committee Turns to Jurisdictional Issues Affecting Proposed Criminal Court'. Committee on International Criminal Court, Resumed First Session, 23rd Meeting (PM). 18 August. Press release L/2738.
—— (1995d). Report of the Ad Hoc Committee on the Establishment of an International Criminal Court. UN Doc. A/50/22.
—— (1996) 'Preparatory Committee on International Criminal Court Concludes First Session'. Press release L/2787. 12 April.
—— (1998). Non-Governmental Organizations Accredited to Participate in the Conference. UN Doc. A/CONF.183/INF/3. 5 June.
—— (2002a). Provisional Record, Security Council, Fifty-seventh year, 4572nd meeting. 12 July. S/PV.4572.
—— (2002b). Security Council Resolution 1422. 12 July.
—— (2003). Provisional Record, Security Council, Fifty-eighth year, 4772nd meeting. 12 June. S/PV.4772.
—— (2004). 'Security Council Extends UN Operation in Burundi until 1 June 2005, Unanimously Adopting Resolution 1577 (2004)'. Press release. 1 December.
United States (1998). 'The Concerns of the United States Regarding the Proposal for a Proprio Motu Prosecutor'. Department of State. 22 June.
—— (2004). 'Eritrea Signs Article 98 Agreement'. State Department press statement, Richard Boucher, spokesman. Washington, DC. 13 July.
'US, Cuba Thumb Down Compromise on Jurisdiction' (1998). *Terra Viva*. 23 June.
'US Launches Long-Awaited Preemptive Strike' (1998), *On the Record*, vol. 1, no. 15. 8 July.
'The US Shows Its Hand'. (1998) *On the Record*, vol. 1, no. 16, part 1. 9 July.
Van Dungen, Peter (1985). *West European Pacifism and the Strategy for Peace*. London: Macmillan.
Van Rooy, Alison (2004). *The Global Legitimacy Game: Civil Society, Globalization, and Protest*. Basingstoke, UK: Palgrave Macmillan.
Von Hebel, Herman (1999). 'An International Criminal Court – a Historical Perspective'. In Herman A. M. von Hebel, Johan G. Lammers and Jolien Schukking (eds), *Reflections on the International Criminal Court: Essays in Honour of Adriaan Bos*. The Hague: T.M.C. Asser Press.
Von Hebel, Herman and Darryl Robinson (1999). 'Crimes within the Jurisdiction of the Court'. In Roy S. Lee (ed.), *The International Criminal Court: The Making of the Rome Statute: Issues, Negotiations, Results*. The Hague: Kluwer Law International.
Von Hebel, Herman, Johan G. Lammers and Jolien Schukking (eds) (1999). *Reflections on the International Criminal Court: Essays in Honour of Adriaan Bos*. The Hague: T.M.C. Asser Press.

Walker, David (1980). *The Oxford Companion to Law*. Oxford: Clarendon Press.

Walker, Rob (1993). *Inside/Outside: International Relations as Political Theory*. Cambridge: Cambridge University Press.

Ware, Alyn (1997). 'Preparatory Committee on the Establishment of an International Criminal Court (ICC PrepCom), December 1–12 1997: Report on War Crimes and Weapons Systems'. http://www.ialana.org/site/affairs/rel_icc.html.

WC (Women's Caucus for Gender Justice in the International Criminal Court) (1997a). *Recommendations and Commentary for August 1997 PrepCom on the Establishment of an International Criminal Court United Nations Headquarters August 4–15, 1997*. August.

—— (1997b). *Recommendations and Commentary for December 1997 PrepCom on the Establishment of an International Criminal Court, United Nations Headquarters December 1–12, 1997*. December.

Weapons Systems Caucus (1997). 'Proposal of the Weapons Systems Caucus'. New York: Weapons Systems Caucus. http://www.ialana.org/site/affairs/index.html.

We the Peoples: Civil Society, the United Nations and Global Governance (2004). Report of the Panel of Eminent Persons on United Nations–Civil Society Relations. UN Doc. A/58/817.

Wedgwood, Ruth (2001). 'The Irresolution of Rome'. *Law and Contemporary Problems*, vol. 64, no. 193 (Winter), pp. 193–214.

'Where Are Decisions Being Made?' (1998). *Terra Viva*. 15 July.

Wilmshurst, Elizabeth (1999). 'Jurisdiction of the Court'. In Roy S. Lee (ed.), *The International Criminal Court: The Making of the Rome Statute: Issues, Negotiations, Results*. The Hague: Kluwer Law International.

Woetzel, Robert Kurt (1960). *The Nuremberg Trials in International Law*. London: Stevens.

Wolf, Val (1997) 'Amnesty International Campaign Update'. *ICC Monitor Special Edition*, p. 11. December.

Women's Initiatives for Gender Justice, in collaboration with Isis-WICCE and Ugandan Women Activists (2004). Press release. 23 November.

Young, Iris Marion (1997). 'Difference as a Resource for Democratic Communication'. In James Bohman and William Rehg (eds), *Deliberative Democracy: Essays on Reason and Politics*. Cambridge, MA: MIT Press.

—— (2001). 'Activist Challenges to Deliberative Democracy'. *Political Theory*, vol. 29, no. 5, pp. 670–690.

Interviews

Bos, Adriaan. Dutch Delegation Leader and Chairman of PrepComs, 26 November 2001.

Burroughs, John. Executive Director, Lawyers Committee on Nuclear Policy, 5 December 2001.

Dicker, Richard. Legal Officer, Human Rights Watch, 6 December 2001.

Donat-Cattin, David. Program Officer for International Law and Human Rights; Former President of the European Law Students Association, 5 December 2001.

Hall Martinez, Katherine. Deputy Director, International Program, Center for Reproductive Law and Policy, 4 December 2001.

Pace, William. Coordinator of the NGO Coalition for an International Criminal Court, 3 and 17 December 2001.

Schabas, William. Professor of Human Rights Law, National University of Ireland, Galway. 27 November 2001.

Van Boven, Theo. Dutch delegation leader to the Rome Conference, 28 November 2001.

Van Troost, Lars. ICC Project Coordinator, Amnesty International, 27 November 2001.

Von Hebel, Herman. Member, Dutch delegation to PrepComs and Rome Conference, 26 November 2001.

Website references

AI (Amnesty International) website: http://www.amnesty.org

AMICC (American Coalition for the International Criminal Court). 'Congressional Update'. http://www.amicc.org/usinfo/congressional.html

Canadian Department of Foreign Affairs and International Trade, 'Canada and the International Criminal Court, History'. http://www.dfait-maeci.gc.ca/foreign_policy/icc/history-en.asp

C-FAM (Catholic Family and Human Rights Institute), http://www.c-fam.org/index.html

CLC (Campaign Life Coalition), http://www.lifesite.net/

Clapham, Andrew, web page at Graduate Institute of International Studies, Geneva. http://heiwww.unige.ch/ens/prof/clapham.html

Fondazione Internationale Lelio Basso, website. http://www.grisnet.it/filb/

Greenpeace website: http://www.greenpeace.org.uk/

HLI (Human Life International), http://www.hli.org/

ICC Monitor, http://www.iccnow.org/publications/monitor.html

ICC website: http://www.icc-cpi.int/, last accessed 1 December 2004.

ICDAA (International Criminal Defence Attorneys Association) website. http://www.hri.ca/partners/aiad-icdaa/

ICFTU (International Confederation of Free Trade Unions) website: http://www.icftu.org/

ICRC (International Committee of the Red Cross) (website). http://www.icrc.org/

Lyonette, Louis-Jacques. 'International Criminal Court: Resources in Print and Electronic Format'. http://www.lib.uchicago.edu/~llou/icc.html.

On the Record: http://www.advocacynet.org/news_view/news_vol_9.html

REAL Women of Canada, http://www.realwomenca.com

Terra Viva, http://www.ips.org/icc/

UNA USA (United Nations Association of the United States of America). 'Frequently Asked Questions about the International Criminal Court'. http://www.unausa.org/programs/qaicc.asp

WICC (Washington Working Group on the International Criminal Court). 'Safeguards for U.S. Personnel under the Rome Treaty for the International Criminal Court'. http://www.wfa.org/issues/wicc/factsheets/safeguards.html

World Federalist Movement. http://www.worldfederalist.org/ABOUT_WFM/About WFM.html

E-mail communications

Perry Robinson, Julian (2004). 'Re: Footnote to Elements of Crimes'. E-mail, 20 August.

Ware, Alyn (2004a). 'Re: Your involvement in the ICC'. E-mail, 23 August.

Ware, Alyn (2004b). 'Trying Again'. E-mail, 23 October.

Personal communication

Manaá, Haytham (2003), Arab Commission on Human Rights. Conversation regarding Arab advocacy on the ICC. Cairo, 23 September.

Index